Letting Go

A FAMILY————
BUSINESS
————PUBLICATION

Family Business Publications are the combined efforts of the Family Business Consulting Group and Palgrave Macmillan. These books provide useful information on a broad range of topics that concern the family business enterprise, including succession planning, communication, strategy and growth, family leadership, and more. The books are written by experts with combined experiences of over a century in the field of family enterprise and who have consulted with thousands of enterprising families the world over, giving the reader practical, effective, and time-tested family business.

D1158890

FBG, founded in 1994, is the leading business consultancy exclusively devoted to helping family enterprises prosper across generations.

FAMILY BUSINESS LEADERSHIP SERIES

This series of books comprises concise guides and thoughtful compendiums to the most pressing issues that anyone involved in a family firm may face. Each volume covers a different topic area and provides the answers to some of the most common and challenging questions.

Titles include:

All of the books were written by members of the Family Business Consulting Group and are based on both our experiences with thousands of client families as well as our empirical research at leading research universities the world over.

Letting Go

*Preparing Yourself to Relinquish
Control of the Family Business*

Craig E. Aronoff

palgrave
macmillan

LETTING GO

Copyright © Family Business Consulting Group, 2003, 2011.

All rights reserved.

First published by the Family Business Consulting Group Publications, 2003.

This edition first published in 2011 by
PALGRAVE MACMILLAN®
in the United States—a division of St. Martin's Press LLC,
175 Fifth Avenue, New York, NY 10010.

Where this book is distributed in the UK, Europe and the rest of the world, this is by Palgrave Macmillan, a division of Macmillan Publishers Limited, registered in England, company number 785998, of Houndmills, Basingstoke, Hampshire RG21 6XS.

Palgrave Macmillan is the global academic imprint of the above companies and has companies and representatives throughout the world.

Palgrave® and Macmillan® are registered trademarks in the United States, the United Kingdom, Europe and other countries.

ISBN: 978–0–230–11115–8

Library of Congress Cataloging-in-Publication Data

Aronoff, Craig E.
    Letting go : preparing yourself to relinquish control of the family business / by Craig E. Aronoff.
        p. cm.—(Family business leadership series)
        Originally published: Marietta, Ga. : Family Enterprise Pub., c2003.
        Includes bibliographical references and index.
        ISBN 978–0–230–11115–8
            1. Family-owned business enterprises—Succession. 2. Executive succession. 3. Family-owned business enterprises—Management.
    4. Family corporations—Management. I. Title.

HD62.25.A7645 2011
658.1'6—dc22   2010045292

A catalogue record of the book is available from the British Library.

Design by Newgen Imaging Systems (P) Ltd., Chennai, India.

First Palgrave Macmillan edition: January 2011

10 9 8 7 6 5 4 3 2 1

Printed in the United States of America.

To my father.

Contents

CONTENTS

Exhibits

Inner Dialogues

Chapter 1

Introduction

The Inner Process of Letting Go

When I was a young consultant and family business leaders asked me for advice on succession planning, I would be very clear on one particular point: "You need to set a date for your retirement, and you need to stick to it." It didn't take me long to realize that I wouldn't have many clients left if I insisted on that idea. While I still think it's good advice, I learned that it didn't fit with a tremendous number of family businesses. And because it didn't, I found that the notion essential to succession, that the incumbent leader will leave the business so that the next generation can take over, needed to be approached in a different way.

"Letting go," means relinquishing control and leadership of a family business, and it is one of the most emotionally difficult experiences of a CEO's life. Few family business owners readily embrace the idea of not being in the position of leadership anymore—with its attendant perks of feeling that one is doing something meaningful, powerful, with prestige in the community and respect from family members. But letting go will occur one way or another. Some business leaders "die with their boots on," staying in power until even their children have retired. Others, are laid low by circumstances—unexpected death, disability, bankruptcy, criminal prosecution and imprisonment, or divorce—not circumstances one would chose as the means of leadership transition. Others are forced out by their boards or their families, often under bitter circumstances. Still others follow a more elegant course, planning years ahead for an orderly transition and mapping out an active, meaningful life for the years after retirement from the family business.

Research shows that about 11 percent of incumbent family business leaders say they will never retire and about 23 percent say they will "semi-retire."[1] That means that a third of all family business leaders aren't going anywhere—they expect to stay in the business.

"Letting go," means relinquishing control and leadership of a family business.

While my bias is for letting go gracefully, I also believe with all my heart in your right, as a family business owner and CEO, to choose. You can hang on, or you can plan your exit. It's your business, and you should be able to do as you please with it.

Whatever path you choose, you must do it responsibly. And that's what this book is all about, helping you make the choice and then implementing it in a way that benefits the business and the family and that gives you satisfaction.

In many respects, this book is a "prequel" to *Family Business Succession: The Final Test of Greatness*. While the earlier book tells you how to plan and manage succession, this book is focused on making yourself ready to do succession planning. It's the preparation here that counts. Planning is relatively easy when the incumbent leader is prepared and virtually impossible when he or she is not.

I see "preparation" as an internal process, one that equips you mentally, emotionally, and perhaps even spiritually for the task ahead—much like a great athlete prepares for a crucial game or race. We'll look at the process from a number of perspectives, but **the key is to begin to understand the extent to which you and your business are separate entities.** In my experience, the greatest difficulties occur when there is a total lack of separation between the individual and the business. Very often, a leader has made an enormous investment in the business in terms of emotion, time, money, thought, and energy, and his or her identity has become rooted in the enterprise. This is true not only of first-generation leaders who started and built the business but also of second- and third-generation CEOs, who see themselves as stewards responsible for a vital legacy. **It is valuable, early on, to understand that you and your organization are separate from each other.**

The greatest difficulties occur when there is a total lack of separation between the individual and the business.

Family business leaders tend not to see retirement as part of a normal career cycle. They are unlike those entrepreneurs who develop an exit strategy as soon as they've started a business. For those who won't let go, life without the business is not something they want to think about. And yet, the single most important factor in the successful transition of a family business to the next generation is the attitude of the person who is sitting in the CEO's chair. If you are that person, that transition depends on you.

This book has been written for you, the incumbent leader. One of its chief goals is to help you become more comfortable with whatever decisions you make about letting go. Just as important, it should enhance your ability to open up dialogues that need to take place with others (and with yourself) about the issues of letting go. It will also help you acquire greater skill in managing the transition process, whether you decide to retire or to stay on as CEO.

Others can benefit from this book as well—your spouse, your sons and daughters, your board of directors, and key non-family members. All are involved in encouraging the generational transition. By better understanding the issues and concerns you face, they can be more supportive in helping you make your way through the inner process of letting go. With increased knowledge, they may gain the courage it takes to engage in the dialogues that are necessary to effective planning.

> The single most important factor in the successful transition of a family business to the next generation is the attitude of the person who is sitting in the CEO's chair.

Succession and retirement are a part of letting go, but effective letting go begins long before these events take place. While you won't find a step-by-step "to do" list in this book, you will gain some new ways of thinking about letting go. You will also encounter some practical ideas and strategies for carrying out the decisions you make. And perhaps most exciting, you can expect to discover some new insights about yourself.

Chapter 2

You Don't "Have" to Retire (but Is Hanging On Worth the Price?)

"This is my business," insists Arnold, the 75-year-old founder and CEO of a family-owned manufacturing company. "I love running it, why should I quit?"

If you're one of those family business leaders who say they're never going to retire, that's okay. You've got lots of company. Like other CEOs, you've devoted your career and the best part of your life to building and sustaining your enterprise—and you've done it for the sake of your family. Running a family-owned company is such an intense experience and so consuming that the business may seem like a beloved child to you. It may have become such an obsession to you that leaving it may seem akin to dying.

But even if you think you've made a firm decision never to retire, maybe it's a decision worth re-examining from time to time. Just as we said you have the right to do what you want with your business, you also have the right to change your mind about not retiring. Along with those rights comes the obligation of communicating with family members and others involved, letting them know where you are in your thinking and giving them an opportunity to discuss it with you. Constant communication over time is essential to the letting-go process, whatever direction it takes.

Arnold, the CEO mentioned above has a son and a daughter working in the business. They are both in their 40s, and each is capable of running the company, but they have finally come to accept the fact that Dad won't let go. While Arnold has tremendous passion for the business, his children have learned to distance themselves psychologically while fulfilling their job responsibilities in the firm. After all, why should they invest themselves so fiercely in the business without being able to affect its direction? They do their jobs competently, but more and more, they have come to regard the business as a financial asset rather than a family legacy. They see it as Dad's toy, and when he can no longer play with it, who knows what will become of it? Arnold's children no longer have a strong emotional stake in keeping it in the family. When Dad is gone, they will probably sell.

Sometimes hanging on is a necessity. There may be no one in the family available to take over, or the anointed successor dies prematurely or becomes incapacitated. An incumbent CEO who can stay on or step back in from retirement for a short period can offer stability to a family firm under unfortunate circumstances. But such situations do suggest that the incumbent has not faced the need to groom a non-family successor on a timely basis, or that depth of management has not been sufficiently developed so that someone is available to step in if the first choice of successor cannot do so.

> Constant communication over time is essential to the letting-go process, whatever direction it takes.

The hazards of hanging on far outweigh letting go. Here are three major ones:

◆ **Your adult children become frustrated and bored.** They feel that they have energies and ideas that are being wasted because they can't be applied. Because they need a challenge, the most competent offspring may leave the business that you say you so much want them to inherit. The least competent will stay because they have no other option.

♦ **Your children become angry and may even become alienated from you.** Still under your thumb, they feel they're not treated as adults and that they're still being told what to do by their parents.

♦ **Your business begins to suffer.** Deprived of the full range of knowledge and skills that your children may have to offer, strategies stagnate and performance erodes. The younger generation, after all, is more in touch with changing trends, developing markets, and shifts in technologies than the older generation is.

WE CAN'T ALL BE RALPH AND BRIAN

Occasionally, business leaders are so energetic and capable that they can make incredible contributions to the family company until well into their 80s or beyond. Ralph Roberts, the cofounder of Comcast Corp., is such a leader. At 82, he played a huge supportive role to his son, Brian, in Comcast's 2002 acquisition of AT&T Broadband, which made Comcast the biggest cable company in the world. Brian, at 43, became chief executive officer, and his father is chairman of the executive committee of the board of directors.

This father and son have a remarkable partnership, in large part because they have exceptional admiration and respect for each other and because Ralph has been able to let go. Brian was named president of Comcast in 1990, when he was 30. Eight years later, Ralph transferred most of the voting stock to Brian.

> The reality is that most CEOs of family businesses need to ask themselves just why it is they intend to hang on.

The *Philadelphia Inquirer* called the Robertses a "storybook father-and-son business team."[2] One observer said their partnership was "one of the most unusual relationships I've seen. I think they are equal in their respect for each other."[3] Following the acquisition of AT&T's cable division, Brian said, "Ralph is still my most trusted confidante, adviser, mentor and partner."[4]

But most of us aren't like Brian and Ralph Roberts. Not many of us have Ralph's willingness to hand over control, and very few of us beyond our 60s have his stamina and brainpower. And few of us are like Brian, a brilliant son born relatively late in his father's life, one who reveres his legendary parent but who is also strong enough and smart enough to work with him as an equal.

WHY AREN'T YOU LETTING GO?

The reality is that most CEOs of family businesses need to ask themselves just why it is they intend to hang on. What keeps them from letting go? A business owner may state some reasons on a conscious level and be very sincere about them. Underneath the surface, however, there may be other reasons that he or she has been unable or unwilling to articulate, or that may even be unrecognized.

Below are reasons that business owners give for not letting go, as well as reasons that family business consultants perceive. Examining them and considering which apply to you should be helpful in considering the extent to which you can separate your identity from the business and see each as a different entity.

"I'm having such a great time!" Business leaders who make this declaration really mean that they don't know what they would do with themselves if they retire. They haven't figured out ways of having fun or finding meaning in life outside the business. And while they may indeed be enjoying themselves, it is likely that they are obstructing an orderly transition of the business to the next generation.

"**I can't afford to retire.**" In the case of certain small businesses, this may actually be true. The business owner needs to continue to work in order to live. But many times, this statement does not reflect reality. Despite having built more than adequate wealth, they still feel financially insecure, or perhaps, the business owner considers the business's financial security more important than his own and will not take resources from the business to afford a comfortable retirement. More about this later.

"**This business would be nothing without me.**" From the perspective of the organization, if there's no successor, there's something wrong. That may not be an issue for the business owner who has essentially built and developed a company in response to his own desires, needs, or beliefs about what needs to be done. His view may be: "This is my business, and whatever's left is for my family to deal with." But, in my view, the owner who does not tend to the needs of the organization is not creating a business. He or she is just self-employed with a lot of helpers. I've worked with such circumstances where the "helpers" ran into the hundreds. With such individuals, there is no sense that "I am creating something to last beyond myself." And when they say, "Without me, this is nothing," they are, sadly, absolutely right.

"**What will I be without the business?**" While a business owner may have convinced himself that the business will be nothing without him, he may also worry more quietly that he will be nothing without the business. He fears losing power, losing prestige in the community, losing the friends and connections that the business affords him, and even losing the respect of his family.

"**I have no successor.**" As suggested above, this can be a legitimate reason for staying on when a successor is suddenly not available as a result of death or disability (or because he changed his mind). This reason can buy time for the incumbent CEO to do what needs to be done to find the management needed to carry on the business. Unfortunately, this is too often an excuse by CEOs whose motive is not to find new leadership but to hang on.

"I want to stay in control of the kids." This is not a reason that a CEO is likely to admit. Entrepreneurs characteristically have a propensity toward control. It helps them do what they do as business creators and builders. But when they try to control their adult children by maintaining control of the business, particularly if it is for his or her own ends and desires, it becomes a serious problem. Some owners disguise this dark desire by saying they're worried their children won't get along without the parent still at the helm.

"I'll die if I retire!" This statement is a favorite of older incumbents. They'll tell you about all the people they know who have retired and died within six months. What they don't tell you is the people they know who have retired and are still alive and well and happy. This comment suggests that the CEO feels he is engaged in an activity that is life-sustaining and that preserves his identity.

"I need to look out for my loyal non-family executives." Family business CEOs commonly have fears about what will happen to their longtime, non-family managers once succession takes place. "These people have taken care of us, and we need to take care of them," many leaders say.

Business owners and the non-family executives often share a significant amount of mutual loyalty. In many cases, they have grown old together. The incumbent leader may worry that if she retires and names a son or daughter as the successor, good non-family executives may get upset at being skipped over. They might leave out of frustration or because they don't want to work for "the kid." Or the founder may be concerned that although the non-family managers worked well with her, they might not work well with the next generation.

Still another concern, in cases where the incumbent leader and his management team have grown old together, is that they all will retire at the same time, making it difficult for the next leader to maintain the business. Instead of planning for such an eventuality, the leader hangs on.

"This business is my life!" The hidden meaning here, perhaps inexpressible for the CEO, is that leaving the business means going home to a marriage that can't survive with both spouses in the house. A number of CEOs throw themselves into their work because they lack other satisfactions in life—including from their spouse and family. They become passionately devoted to their business, and it becomes their "mistress." Retirement will have serious consequences on other parts of a CEO's life. In some cases, it can result in such a traumatic shock to the marital system that the CEOs marriage does not survive. CEOs who recognize this as their own situation may keep on working because they don't want to face the probability of a divorce. This sadness and loneliness can be reality to some. The fortunate CEO recognizes such potential difficulties early in life and seeks help from a marriage and family therapist. Such problems are beyond the scope of this book, but if the prospect of your marriage collapsing is preventing you from implementing a succession in your business, you may want to consider seeing a counselor.

Another complicating factor is that entrepreneurs tend to be fundamentally insecure. On the plus side, their insecurity makes them vigilant. It keeps them working hard and makes them take their responsibilities very seriously. It gives them the drive to succeed. On the other hand, however, it renders them perpetually worried about the status of their organization and what might happen tomorrow. It feeds their anxieties, and the anxieties, in turn, provide fodder for not letting go when letting go is the best way to go.

Very often what keeps a CEO from letting go is the need for security.

WHAT'S HOLDING YOU BACK?

Many CEOs really do want to hand the business over to the next generation but just don't know how to go about it. If you are one of them, please see *Family Business Succession: The Final Test of Greatness*. The first book in the Family Business Leadership Series is a step-by-step guide to planning and managing succession.

Very often, however, what keeps a CEO from letting go is the need for security in four areas:

1. **Personal financial security.** ("Do my spouse and I have the resources to live comfortably the rest of our lives?")
2. **Family security.** ("I'm afraid the family will fall apart if I relinquish my leadership position.")
3. **Organizational security.** ("Can the business function without me?")
4. **Psychological security.** ("If I'm not the CEO of this company, who am I? And what am I going to do?")

In my experience, once business owners achieve a comfort zone in each of these areas, they can move on to the tasks of

---

EXHIBIT 1   **Nine Reasons (or Excuses?) Why CEOs Hang On**

1. "I'm having a great time!"
2. "I can't afford to retire."
3. "This business is nothing without me."
4. "I might be nothing without the business."
5. "I have no successor."
6. "I want to be able to control the kids through the business."
7. "If I retire, I'll die!"
8. "I need to look out for my loyal non-family executives."
9. "My marriage might fail if I retire."

planning and implementing succession. You will find more about these security needs and how to fill them in Chapter 5.

KNOWING WHEN TO LET GO

For some family business CEOs, knowing when to let go comes easy. They've lost the desire to run the business. They aren't motivated by it anymore. They want to do something else with their lives. Or, long ago, they set a retirement date and they are sticking to it.

CEOs who are reluctant to retire, however, may be in danger of ignoring the signs that it is time for them to hand leadership over to the next generation. If you are in this group, here are some questions that you should periodically ask yourself and answer as honestly as you can:

1. Is my company losing good people?
2. Is it losing its competitive advantage?
3. Am I losing focus? When there are problems, do I know what needs to be done to correct them?
4. How is my stamina? Am I still willing to dig in, or am I beginning to throw up my hands when things get tough?
5. Is my motivation still strong?
6. Do I still have the ability to run this company, or has it outgrown my skills and knowledge? Do I increasingly have to turn to younger people to deal with problems beyond my understanding?
7. Am I still having fun?
8. What feedback am I getting? Is anyone suggesting, however gently, that it's time for me to hang it up or that my successor is ready to take over?

I've seen CEOs in their late 50s step out of the leadership role and pass it on, very appropriately, to the next generation. I've also seen CEOs who at 65 are absolutely vigorous, healthy, and alert and have mastered computer basics, yet choose to let go. They're saying, "It's time. My kids are ready, and it is inappropriate for me to stay on when they're fully prepared to take over just because I feel like I still have something that I want to do." Such CEOs are often second- or third-generation owners who had a parent who wouldn't let go and who remember how agonizing the business succession process was. "I remember what my father did to me, and I'm not going to do the same thing to my kids," they often say.

CEOs who let go willingly are, in many ways, selfless people. They are people who are committed to the generations to come. They are people who put the family and the institution that they have created or served above themselves. They have faced down the fear that retirement leads to death because they know there are many, many role models that prove otherwise. In my estimation, they are completely admirable.

CEOs who let go willingly are, in many ways, selfless people.

DO YOU REALLY OWN A FAMILY BUSINESS?

As the CEO, you must ask yourself whether or not you are really committed to succession and to preserving the business for future generations. If you have what you proudly describe as a family firm, **then you must be concerned about letting go, and you must be concerned about the business surviving beyond you.** To be consistent with the declaration that you have a family business, to be honest about it, and in order to fulfill your responsibilities as a family business leader, you must accept the "final test of greatness" and recognize that handing the business off to your successor is your key challenge.

In other words, a family business is truly a family business only when it is successfully passed from one generation to another. Such a transition is usually the most satisfactory when the CEO plans for it and steps back from the business when the next generation is ready to take over. But if your decision is to hang on, you can also take steps to assure an orderly transition when ill health or death decides your tenure is over. Ways to hang on responsibly are discussed in detail in Chapter 9.

A family business is truly a family business only when it is successfully passed from one generation to another.

INNER DIALOGUE

What about Me and My Spouse?

If I Stay On	If I Let Go
She has her life and I have mine, and mine has always been the business. What will happen if I am no longer running the company?	She'll still have her life, and I'll have a chance to develop new interests of my own. There are also things we've talked about doing together—like community theater.
I know she doesn't want me at home, underfoot. Staying on keeps me safely out of her domain.	It'll be hard, but I'll have to resist the temptation to take over running the house. I'll have to keep busy.
We don't talk to each other much anymore, except about the kids, the grandkids, and the business. As long as I'm working, it's no big deal.	What will we talk about? This is a tough one. Maybe it's not too late to get counseling for our communication problems.
She can continue to enjoy the prestige and respect that comes with being the CEO's wife.	She'll miss the "perks" of being the boss's spouse. We'll need to find some trade-offs that will make this loss worthwhile.
If I stay on, I don't have to face these issues.	I think she and I are both willing to deal with these challenges.

Chapter 3

Whose Decision Is It Anyway?

In the world of publicly traded businesses, CEOs typically don't have the option of hanging on. A company policy mandates retirement age or a board of directors tells them it's time to go. Even Jack Welch, hailed by some as the greatest corporate manager of the 20th century, bowed out of General Electric at the conventional retirement age of 65.

In the world of family business, however, a great number of CEOs—perhaps a majority—have the option of making the decision themselves as to when or whether they will retire. And because they have that option, it's very important for them to engage in the internal process of letting go—important for themselves and important to the organization that he or she leads.

On the whole, it's more effective and pleasant for all concerned if the incumbent can truly let go by virtue of his own decision as opposed to having to be pushed out the door. Gail Ludewig, president and CEO of TotalWorks, Inc., a Chicago publishing company, told the *Wall Street Journal* how difficult it was to get her father, the second-generation owner, to let go. In 1997, he split the ownership of the company three ways with Ms. Ludewig, her brother, and himself. While the company thrived under Ms. Ludewig's leadership, her father, who was supposed to be working in sales while he prepared for retirement, continued to try to involve himself in daily operations, asking questions and becoming upset if he wasn't given a part in decision making. Ms. Ludewig said she found the behavior "disruptive." What's more, their management styles clashed.

In 2000, when he was 73, Ms. Ludewig's father finally agreed to retire and to let his son and daughter buy out his share of the business over a ten-year period. However, Ms. Ludewig wanted to be sure there was a physical break as well. When a layout was created for new offices later that year, Ms. Ludewig deliberately did not include office space for her dad and took it upon herself to break the news to him.[5]

Most likely, you don't want to go to your business one day and find out that the kids have made your letting-go decision for you by removing your desk and chair. Nor do you want to experience a family "intervention," where all your family members come together and confront you, insisting that you must retire in much the same way that other families confront a member about addiction or the need to give up the car keys. And in all probability, you don't want the grim reaper making the decision for you, even though some business owners choose that option. As one of them said: "God is our human resources director. He makes the retirement policy."

Fortunately, however, there are other scenarios.

CREATING AN INTELLIGENT PROCESS

Many incumbent CEOs have a hard time recognizing when it's time to go, even when they're miserable. If you're the founder, you've been totally wrapped up in the business, nurturing its growth and struggling to keep it going. If you inherited leadership and see yourself as a steward, you've learned to put your own feelings aside and soldier on. You may be 70 years old and unhappy, but your instincts are to "dig in." Most people who feel miserable realize that something's got to change. A CEO outside a family business would be saying, "I think it's time for me to hang it up. I need somebody else to take this over." However, a family business leader's reaction may be, "I've got to hunker down and try harder. I've got to recommit myself."

Even though the decision of when and how to retire may rest in the incumbents' hands, thoughtful CEOs often choose to turn the decision over to others.

Frequently, CEOs live for their work and pour themselves into it. Such CEOs are the ones most likely to demand that they have the right to decide personally when they will retire. They are also the least likely to be able to make that decision from anything other than their own perspective. Given the obsession with the business that can exist and the probable lack of objectivity, leaving the decision to the incumbent CEO can be dangerous to the health of the enterprise and those within it.

Even though the decision of when and how to retire may rest in the incumbents' hands, thoughtful CEOs often choose to turn the decision over to others. They know there's more to life than work and are actually looking forward to engaging in other kinds of activities. They may also be very conscious of the younger people who are coming up through the ranks and want to give them the fullest opportunities for responsibility and authority as soon as they are ready to accept it.

They understand that their retirement decision is not simply personal—not just about themselves. It is also an organizational decision. On a personal level, they think about such questions as, "Who am I? What do I want? How do I fulfill my needs?" The organizational decisions they think about are: "How do we create a living organization? How do we have accountability? What kinds of systems do we need? How do we structure our organization?"

These wise CEOs also ask themselves some key questions: "Am I really the best judge of my own performance? Will I be

truly capable of deciding by myself when I am ready to retire? Or shall we create a process where that's decided by others?"

In many cases, the prudent CEO turns to the company board of directors and says, "Retirement is not my decision. It's your decision." Typically, the board can consider either when the incumbent "doesn't have it anymore" or when the successor is ready to assume responsibility—or a combination of the two. What boards usually do is continuously put pressure on the executives of the organization to attend to developing their successors.

In another scenario, the CEO enlists the help of others, such as family shareholders and key managers, to develop a policy that governs the decision. Perhaps the policy mandates retirement at 65 for all in the company, including the CEO. Sometimes, a family business puts the decision into the hands of the board of directors, which may also be guided by a policy but which may have some flexibility in implementing it.

What boards usually do is continuously put pressure on the executives of the organization to attend to developing their successors.

When the decision is subjected to others in an intelligent process, chances are it will be more objective, less personal, and less emotional. It will better serve the interests of the business, and it will relieve the CEO's children of the pain and ambiguity of having to deal with a reluctant retiree or of pushing him or her out the door. The CEO in turn won't have to experience being shoved out of the way by ambitious offspring. She can say, "Our company policy requires that I retire three years from now when I'm 65. My daughter has been well prepared, and she'll be ready to take over then."

INNER DIALOGUE

Who Am I?

If I Am CEO	If I Am NOT CEO
I enjoy my work. I can't imagine life without it.	I can finally do all the other things I've wanted to do—start another business, sit on some volunteer boards, and travel.
I have the satisfaction of building a wonderful company, something that will be my legacy.	I have built a company capable of living without me. That's a kind of immortality.
My name is well known. I have tremendous prestige in my community and in my industry.	As CEO, my son will carry on the prestige of our family name in the community and in our industry.
I have a useful outlet for my energy, my creativity, and my vision.	I can use my energy and ability in other venues besides the business. It'll be fulfilling and fun.
My family respects me.	My family respects me.
I enjoy a great deal of control and influence—in my business, my community, and my family.	I don't need to be in control all the time. I'll still be respected—especially when I recognize that others are just as capable as I am.
I want to stay on.	I'm looking forward to other adventures.

Chapter 4

Taking People Hostage

"Just hold on and be patient. Your time will come."
"I'm going to retire one of these days. I just haven't decided when."
"Someday this will all be yours."

Sound familiar? These are the kinds of statements CEOs make when they don't want to retire but they do want to keep their children in the business. In other words, they take the kids psychologically captive.

Contrast the statements above with the CEO who gathered his sons and daughters to explain to them his intentions to hang on as long as he could. "You are welcome to stay in the business or if you see better opportunities to take them. I won't love you any less." This CEO was honest with himself and his family. Rather than manipulating or obfuscating, he paints a clear picture of the choices available and blesses whichever course they chose. That's very different from an aging CEO controlling the family by controlling the business. In telling their adult children exactly what to do and expecting them to respond obediently, they are controlling and infantilizing their sons and daughters.

Why don't the children just leave? Some of the strongest do, but the separation can be painful and injurious to family relationships. Others, at least for a while, believe it when their parent-CEOs tell them that the business "will be yours to run one day. Just hold on a little longer." That day can keep receding, stretching into decades. Promises, guilt, money, perks, and prestige can be used to maintain the children's involvement in the business and their dependence on it and on their parents.

A CEO might say, "You can leave the business, but if you do, you'll be cut out of my will." One business founder even stipulated in his will that ownership of his very successful business would pass only to those of his offspring working in the business at the time of his death. A spouse can collude with the CEO, such as a wife who says to a son or daughter, "If you leave the business it'll kill your father!" The children, in effect, are not psychologically free to make decisions about their own lives and careers. In my experience, such families have little success in sustaining businesses across generations or in building productive, fulfilling lives.

WHAT HOSTAGES CAN DO

When sons and daughters in such situations call me, what I tell them is to sit tight and wait it out knowing that time is on their side, and they will most likely outlast their aging parent. The alternative is to establish their independence by leaving the business and setting out on their own.

Many of the best leave, because they can. They have the talent to find good opportunities elsewhere.

If you decide to leave, try to do so without burning bridges. Establish your independence but do it with love and respect. Say things like:

♦ "I'm going out to do my own thing. I've moved up to the point where I feel like I'm ready to lead a business. But clearly that chance is not available to me here because you're still running this company."

♦ "We've tried to work together on this issue, but we still don't see eye to eye. So I am going to go out, and I'm going to pursue some other opportunities. You're my dad. I love you. I understand the situation."

♦ "I don't resent you about your decision. I appreciate all you've done for me. If I've reached the point where I'm ready to run a business—and I think I have—it's because of the education that you've financed and the experience that you've helped me get. But I'm leaving for a while. Let's keep talking all the time, and when you're ready, if you want, maybe I'll come back. Maybe I'll build a business that we can merge into this one. Maybe we can work together on some joint ventures. So this isn't necessarily forever, but it's something that I need to do now."

Occasionally, talk like this loosens the incumbent's position. He says, "Oh my, what am I doing? Is this what I really want?" Reassessing the circumstances and relationships, the CEO may conclude, "Okay. I'm going to back off," and tries to do that. He may make himself chairman and make the son or daughter CEO. But like Gail Ludewig and her father, struggles over power and control are likely to continue.

EXHIBIT 2   **CEOs Hold Kids Captive When They...**

- Say they'll retire but they never do it
- Stall sons and daughters about succession
- Make promises about succession but don't keep them
- Use guilt to keep their children from leaving the business
- Threaten to cut heirs out of the will if they don't stay in the business

Chapter 5

Make It Easy on Yourself

B ecause the preparations for letting go can take as much as a decade or more, CEOs are well advised to get started when they are still in their 40s. Charles Collat, the second-generation leader of Mayer Electric Supply, Inc., in Birmingham, Alabama, had begun thinking about letting go but didn't engage in the process in earnest until he was 60, when he called in a family business consultant to help. Still, it took a decade to effect a successful transition, and Collat was 70 when he finally retired.

ACHIEVING SECURITY

Earlier in this book, we touched on the need to achieve security in four areas: the business organization, personal finances, family relationships, and personal psychological security. CEOs have a hard time letting go if they feel uneasy about any of these factors. You can make letting go easier on yourself when you do the hard work necessary to attain security and feelings of well-being and comfort about each of these issues. And you make it easier on yourself when you start this work earlier rather than later. When you start early, you avoid the pressure and stress and frustration that result from waiting until the last minute. Instead, you provide yourself the time necessary to thoughtfully and diligently accomplish what you need to. Generally, in my experience, once a CEO hits age 60 or 65, it's really hard to make the letting-go process work.

Let's consider the four areas of security one by one.

1. Organizational Security

The question is: do you have a viable company? Is it sound enough to run without you? Whether you let go or hang on, the time will come when you are not there to run your family business. Your responsibility is to make it ready so that it can sustain itself once you're gone.

But perhaps you already have a company that can succeed on its own. I've worked with many CEOs of very successful companies who have very earnestly said, "You have no idea how fragile this business is." They feel sure they are the only thing standing between the continuation of an enterprise and its demise, when in fact the organization is just fine. Business owners sometimes fail to recognize that they have a viable company even when they do. If you have an effective board, it can help to assess your business's health. Perhaps you should hire a business consultant to provide an honest, objective assessment of the condition of your business and, if necessary, to make recommendations for bringing it up to snuff. The professional assessment will give you reassurance and more peace of mind. Perhaps only a little fine tuning is needed. But if the organization really does need a major overhaul, now you'll know and you can prepare accordingly.

Family business consulting pioneer Léon Danco has described one type of organization chart as "The Rake," with the boss at the top and the help at the bottom—something like the self-employed individual with a lot of helpers mentioned earlier. One family business CEO called me and said, "I have two sons in the business, and I want them to move up through the organization and succeed me." After studying the company, I told him there was a big problem: "You don't have any organization for them to move up through." While he had a number of key non-family executives, he had no vice presidents and took the attitude that "titles don't mean anything." What the lack of titles really meant was that his executives had neither the responsibility nor the authority to make decisions without checking with the CEO first. With my encouragement, he soon named three vice presidents and began to back off from involving himself in all the decisions. Not only did the non-family executives at last have a sense that they could move up in the company, but the new structure also provided a clearer career path for the sons if they chose to pursue succeeding their father. The CEO was now on the way to developing people who could make the decisions necessary to keeping the business going when he was out of the picture.

The successful transition of your business to the next generation will come about not because you focus on succession and retirement but because you focus on building a solid organization.

Your formal, established goal should be to get the organization ready to live without you. That means establishing structures and processes for accountability, communication, planning, and decision making. When CEOs do this, they eventually find that their organization can function without them. It's a revelation to them, one that eases the letting-go process tremendously.

The successful transition of your business to the next generation will come about not because you focus on succession and retirement but because you focus on building a solid organization. If you don't, the business will remain dependent on you, giving you every reason not to let go.

Some actions that are helpful in shaping a viable organization include:

◆ **Create a good system for gathering solid financial information.** Report it in meaningful ways to the appropriate people. Too many CEOs carry vital information around in their heads, depriving others of the information they need to run the organization effectively if the CEO is not available. Having a good system for gathering and sharing information doesn't just empower others to pick up and run the business. If you become chairman, it will also enable you to look at the numbers and have a good sense of what's going on, strengthening your ability to provide oversight to the business as a whole.

◆ **Hire a top-notch management team.** Depending on the size of your business, recruit two or three of the most experienced, brilliant people you can find. Yes, you'll have to pay top dollar, but first-class performers will increase your company's profit by much more than they earn. I've seen too many family business owners hire "cheap" instead of hiring good, or hire for loyalty instead of for ability. Resist those temptations. **Hire people better than yourself, give them responsibility, and coach them to work as a team.** When you do, you'll feel much better about your organization and more secure about letting go of it.

It's also helpful to layer management in a variety of ages. It's fairly common for family business CEOs to be surrounded by key non-family executives about their own age. But when such a CEO is ready to retire, so is his management team. Really thoughtful CEOs make sure there are key executives not only in the CEO's own age group, but also some in their 50s, 40s, and even 30s. Doing so assures a continuity of management for the future.

◆ **Establish an outside board of directors**—that is, a board that includes two or more directors who are not family members, employees, friends, or advisors (lawyer, banker, etc.). The best outside directors are often CEOs of other companies. Such a board can choose and help develop the leadership successor, assure that the CEO is accountable, and advise on and support business strategy.

◆ **Draft a job description for the CEO.** I encourage CEOs to write a job description that outlines the role and sets forth the duties of the next CEO and therefore defines what is needed in the successor. This is a useful exercise on several fronts. If you are CEO and owner and chairman, you are probably doing some things that really aren't CEO work. You may be doing them because you are the owner, but they may be responsibilities that could be delegated to a vice president or someone else. Creating a CEO's job description not only clarifies what the CEO should be doing and what the business needs in its next leader but also opens up developmental opportunities for other people in the organization. As these people gain skills and experience, the business becomes stronger.

Here is one example of a CEO's job description. (The chairman's role is addressed in Chapter 8.)

EXHIBIT 3   Position Description: President and Chief Executive Officer

I. BASIC FUNCTION
To provide leadership that enables the Corporation to develop excellence and grow profitably, by upholding the principles of the Corporation and by serving as the firm's senior operational leader.

II. RESPONSIBILITY AND AUTHORITY
Subject to applicable provisions of the Certificate of Incorporation, the bylaws and the limits from time to time established by the Board of Directors, is responsible for managing the business, the property, and the affairs of the Corporation. The President and CEO is the single individual responsible for the overall successful administration of the daily affairs of the Corporation.

A. Leadership Vision

1. Maintains a continuous emphasis on personal growth and development of people, always rewarding and promoting the loyal, the most qualified, and the individuals most likely to succeed.

2. Develops and disseminates throughout the Corporation a basic philosophy of stewardship, equity, and consideration for all customers, suppliers, employees, and investors. Contributes to the development and growth of fellow employees, and by word and deed supports and promotes Corporate Principles.
3. Sets an example of diligence in work and persistence in pursuing and exceeding planned performance.
4. Represents the Corporation to the public and to customers in such a way as to enhance its reputation.
5. Works with the Chairman in maintaining and directing family and shareholder relations that so the shareholders' confidence in the Corporation is strengthened and their values are pursued.

B. Planning

1. Initiates, in consultation with the Chairman and Executive Committee, short-range and long-range business planning that will establish objectives, define strategy, and describe the operational implementation steps necessary.
2. Develops strategic planning methods and policies and ensures their effective implementation.
3. Initiates planning for expansion into new markets and with new products. Submits recommendations and status reports at quarterly review with the Executive Committee.
4. With Board of Director approval and direction, manages all investigations and negotiations pertaining to mergers, acquisitions, joint ventures, and/or disposal of major assets.
5. Assists in planning activities at the Board, Executive Committee, and Family Council levels.

C. Organization

1. Develops and maintains an organizational plan and structure that will maximize the contribution, skills, and talent of individuals within the Corporation and that will support the accomplishment of the Corporation's objectives. Submits for annual review by the Board Personnel Committee.

2. Internally identifies and/or recruits, develops, and trains individuals to assume leadership positions within the management team.
3. Directs a management development program that will enable the Corporation to meet its projected management personnel needs.
4. Establishes and maintains an effective system of communication throughout the company and assures that barriers to effective communication are minimized.

D. Controls

1. Ensures the development and maintenance of standards of accountability and reporting to ensure regular and accurate review of activities and performance.
2. Maintains regular reporting and evaluation sessions for each individual reporting to the President/CEO position.
3. Initiates and reviews the management of systems and programs to assure maximum customer retention.
4. Initiates and maintains standards and procedures for decision making and improved profit margins, reporting annually to the Finance Committee.
5. Develops and maintains a personal awareness and understanding of the various levels of operations.

E. Decision Making

1. Delegates, by the use of appropriate policies and procedures, authority for decision making to that level or position in the organization where such decisions can be made most competently and intelligently for the benefit of customer service, quality, and profitability.
2. Recommends actions to the Chairman for consideration by the Board or its committees and participates in decision making at both levels.

F. Climate

1. Develops confidence and respect among employees of the organization by maintaining modes of conduct that encourage an environment of mutual respect and trust.

2. Establishes a team of leaders among those reporting to the President/CEO that promotes the corporate culture of customer-oriented performance, respect in the workplace, and fair recognition for individual and group accomplishments.
3. Maintains personal involvement with the various segments of the organization and its representatives, dealers, suppliers, friends, and customers in order to be currently informed and involved in the basic problems and potentials of the business, and to promote cooperative, customer-oriented working relationships.

III. ACCOUNTABILITY

A. Develops clear objectives and goals and reports these to the Board, and establishes goals and standards of performance for those reporting to the President/CEO.
B. Preserves and expands the base of existing resources and directs aggressive growth within a framework consistent with the policies, directives, and resolutions of the Board of Directors. Reports quarterly changes in resources to Finance and Personnel Committees.
C. Optimizes and balances long-range and short-range results in growth, profitability, and continuity together with service to society and opportunity for all employees.
D. Represents the company with major customers, the financial community, attorneys, government agencies, other outside advisors and professional groups, and the media.

IV. ORGANIZATIONAL RELATIONSHIPS

A. Reports to the Board of Directors
B. Reporting to the President/CEO are:
    1. Executive VP Operations
    2. Chief Financial Officer
    3. Senior VP Marketing
    4. Senior VP Research and Development

5. Senior VP Human Resources
6. Division Vice Presidents

Reprinted with permission from Beryl Loomis. Additional material in this position description was provided by Norbert E. Schwarz of the Family Business Consulting Group, Inc.

Family Business Succession: The Final Test of Greatness offers a detailed discussion on preparing the business and developing successors.

2. Personal Financial Security

The fundamental question is, "How much is enough?" And that question has two parts: "How much is enough for the incumbent CEO and spouse for the rest of their lifetimes?" and, "How much is enough for the business?" Addressing the issue of personal financial security necessitates considering the business's financial security as well, since one impacts the other. It also means looking at your estate planning and reflecting on what you want to do and how you want to live in your retirement years.

If you're committed to the idea that your business is a family business, intended to be passed on to the next generation, then you need to look at your personal financial picture in that context. Can you meet the goal of financing a secure retirement for yourself and still pass on a viable business to your children? Or will your personal financial needs and desires result in underinvesting in the business and failing to make needed strategic change or to take appropriate business risks? If the latter, you may feel more personally financial secure but, in the long term, you may jeopardize the health and viability of the business reducing its ability to be passed on to the next generation.

A key to effective succession, however, is proactive planning to provide lifetime financial security for the older generation. And the earlier it starts, the better. As one financial planner put it: "Good planning for retirement takes a lifetime."

In general, it's best if the CEO and spouse start early and build financial security outside the business. Here's an excellent guideline: **if you save and conservatively invest 10 percent of your income every year for 20 to 25 years, you will be able to assure yourself a full income for life without selling or controlling the business.** Granted, this takes years of planning and saving, plus great discipline and foresight. But there are many advantages: Business decisions needn't be driven by the need for personal income. You put yourself in a position to transfer your shares with maximum tax advantage to the next generation. You even set a good example for the next generation, which also needs to start saving as early as possible.

Maybe 10 percent is not the right figure. Depending on your aspirations for retirement, you may need to set aside more. If you look forward to a life of gardening, reading, and writing, with just a little travel thrown in, your needs will be minimal. But if you expect to add substantially to your art collection of modern masters, traveling the world to do so, "what's enough" will be a much higher figure. Perhaps you want to be an "angel" investor, providing venture capital to startup companies. That's an activity that could be conducted within or outside your business, depending on its strategy and situation and on whether or not funds are available and whether or not they can be moved outside the company.

A key to effective succession is proactive planning to provide lifetime financial security for the older generation.

Another post-retirement goal might be involvement in philanthropy. As the CEO, you might have engaged in philanthropy under the aegis of the business, making gifts to the community and its institutions. If philanthropy is your passion, it might be time to separate that activity from the business and continue it as an individual, possibly creating a private foundation or putting money into a donor-advised fund where you can offer direction (but not control) on how the money is used.

Money can be transferred out of the business for such purposes in ways that do not have tax consequences.

As you develop and implement a personal financial security plan, estate plans, and plans for your post-retirement life, you'll want to turn to others for input. Invite your children to make their own desires clear and to raise any concerns they have for you to consider. Your key managers and board of directors can help you think through the capital needs of the business and the impact any of your choices will have on the company and vice versa. Your professional advisors can offer specific advice on the legal and tax aspects of the options you are considering.

One final bit of advice: **be generous with yourself, within the context of the overall health of your business.**

You've worked long and hard, made great sacrifices, and achieved admirably. You deserve your financial reward and to feel the next generation's appreciation for the opportunity you've afforded them.

Let your children grow up.

While you have to be realistic about the business's health, all too often CEOs feel they can only take enough money out of a company "to live on," even though they would like to engage in "angel" investing, philanthropy, or other more costly endeavors. They're used to being concerned about the business having sufficient capital and have kept it conservatively financed over the years. And even though it may be overcapitalized, they are reticent to take funds out. "We need to keep the money in the business to keep it healthy," they say. What they don't realize is that if they don't take this money out of the business, there's a high probability that the business won't stay healthy because of the continued tenure of an increasingly financially conservative leader—who won't let go because he does not feel personally financially secure enough to do so.

3. Family Security

Let your children grow up. That's the essence of achieving family security in a family business, but it's very hard to do. A business owner we'll call Mark, now the chairman of a Midwest plastics extrusion firm, recently promoted a non-family executive, Ben, to the CEO post. Mark would really love for his 34-year-old son, Sam, to be named to Ben's old post as division chief, but it's clear to everyone but Sam himself that he is not ready for the responsibility. Meanwhile, Ben is trying to do his old job plus his new one and can't give adequate attention to either.

What parents must do is to have adult expectations of their children and apply the same criteria to their sons and daughters that they do to other employees.

Mark and his wife keep hoping their son will soon be ready for the promotion. Ben, however, would like to hire an outsider for the vacancy. He's convinced Sam will never be ready for the job and says, "Sam is bright enough to do this job, but he's not focused or disciplined. He's not developing his own priorities or showing leadership to the other people in the organization." In Ben's view, Sam should be able to develop focus and discipline himself. He's right, but Sam hasn't done so because his parents have never said to him, "If you don't do it, you're through. You're not going to make it." Instead they say, "Keep trying. You'll make it someday."

Sam's parents, like many family business couples, are seeking to protect their son from failure. They are trying to engineer the circumstances that will allow their son's success as opposed to making Sam responsible for his own achievement. What parents must do, instead, is to have adult expectations of their children and apply the same criteria to their sons and daughters that they do to other employees. They must demand that their children present their plans, their views, their expectations, and their intention for where the business is going to go and how they are going to work effectively with one another.

Many family business parents find it tough to face reality as it relates to their children. By not letting go, CEOs and their spouses are able to maintain a kind of status quo that allows them not to deal with the facts of the situation. Reality here may mean you need to pick one of your children over other children to be the successor, or find a way that such a choice can be accomplished (by a board of directors, for example). Reality may also mean that one or more of your children shouldn't be in the business and should be encouraged to find work outside it. Or perhaps some of your children just don't get along and you desperately want them to. Factors like these tempt incumbent CEOs to hang on, either to protect their children or to prevent them from blowing up at one another.

Such CEOs have laudable motives. "I don't want to hurt my children," they say. Or, "I want my children to be happy." Or, "I want my children to feel successful." It's the classical dilemma of parenting, which is: you've got to take the training wheels off and, when you do, the bicycle's going to fall down and your child is going to scrape his knees. In a family business, however, the stakes are higher.

It may sometimes appear that the business is going to be injurious to the family because it is impossible for it to meet every family member's need. Not every child can be CEO. Not every child may be able to work in the business. Not every child can be treated equally in a family firm (although all CAN be treated fairly, in both the business and the family). But encountering and rising above disappointment is a part of growing up—for children of family business CEOs as for everybody else.

For that reason, I urge parents not to protect their children or give them special treatment in the family business. It does them no favor. In several businesses I know, the CEOs have created what are essentially make-work jobs for children who they believe are unable to support themselves. In one, a simple subsidiary was created to supply the family business with lawn maintenance services, and a son was put in charge of it. The young man thinks he's running a business when, in fact, he does not have to go out and seek any customers, he does not have to compete with anybody, and he does not even have to hire anyone because his father transferred a few employees from the family firm to the lawn company. It's all an illusion. Unfortunately, the son has never had to face reality, basic to most people, of having to find a job. And now he is being deprived by a protective father-CEO from the kinds of experiences that would enable him to become truly an adult.

Parents owe their children the opportunity to stumble and pick themselves up. When CEOs see that their children are made of "sterner stuff' and can cope with difficult adult responsibilities and relationships, they begin to feel more confident about the family and more reassured that when they let go, their businesses will be in good hands, and the family won't fall apart.

On the other hand, if you are the son or daughter of a CEO who is reluctant to retire and you really want him out of there, is it possible that you are contributing to his reluctance? We'll take a look at this possibility in the next chapter, "The Supporting Cast."

4. Personal Psychological Security

In many respects, this whole book is about achieving the personal psychological security that enables you, as CEO, to let go of an institution that has been very dear to you for most of your adult life. When you have spent so many years so closely intertwined with your business, it is very hard to separate your identity from that of your company. Yet, that is something that must be done so that you can discover who you are apart from the business and what can make you happy when you let go.

Let's suppose you are in your 60s or even 70s. You've succeeded beyond all expectations in creating or growing a business. You are financially comfortable. **Why are you still working?** Family business CEOs who have trouble letting go really have to look inward and seriously answer that question for themselves.

When you ask yourself why you are still hanging on, that leads you to other important questions: What are my motives?

What am I working for? What are my goals? Am I doing this for reasons that relate to myself, or am I still working for reasons that relate to the business as a whole? If I'm doing it for reasons as they relate to the business, why haven't we been able to solve these problems earlier? And shouldn't we now be devoting ourselves to that? If I'm doing it for myself, am I being honest about that, and am I communicating my position to others? Who am I—particularly if I'm not part of this business?

Gaining personal psychological security means not being afraid to ask basic questions of yourself and of others who can help you acquire insight into yourself. It is extremely helpful to seek counseling from or at least conversation with others: family; friends; or professionals such as psychologists, consultants, clergy, executive coaches, and the like. They can draw you out with questions of their own and, as appropriate, offer observations about you that might help you think about yourself in new ways.

Gaining personal psychological security means not being afraid to ask basic questions of yourself and of others who can help you acquire insight into yourself.

Hard-charging entrepreneurs and CEOs are often people who throughout their lives have tended to think it's a weakness to own up to feelings. **At this stage of life, however, it's important to accept one's own feelings, to probe them, and to deal with them.** When people can't do that, they're going to have problems achieving psychological security.

THE ULTIMATE ISSUE

Relinquishing control is the ultimate letting-go issue. You haven't really let go until you have given up not only your job-title responsibilities but also released voting control. At some point, it is extremely appropriate to let go of voting stock. You either conclude that the issues that concern you have been adequately resolved or that your continued input is probably standing in the way of a resolution.

If you have satisfactorily addressed the four security issues discussed above but still haven't let go of the voting stock, it's very possible that you have what most of us would call a "control problem." In that case, you can try to overcome it, perhaps with professional counseling, or you can say the heck with it and hang on to your business. If the latter is your choice, pay close attention to Chapter 9, "What If You Choose to Hang On?"

NO HEROES, PLEASE

Letting go requires you to be very counterintuitive to your own needs. Just when you need reassurance about and recognition for what you've accomplished, you also need to deflect credit to others. Doing so is best both for the business and the family.

As you get older, you are very likely asking such questions as: "What does it all mean? What have I contributed?" It's natural to want recognition for your achievements—the plaques on the wall, the award ceremonies, and the appreciation dinners. Appreciation is a normal part of the retirement process, and it's not wrong to want it and to enjoy it. Nevertheless, as their lives move in this direction, some very farsighted and thoughtful entrepreneurs deliberately de-emphasize and de-mythologize themselves. **Instead of letting people credit them as individuals—for their creativity, their brilliance, or their exceptional talents—they shift the credit to the company team and the organization's principles and values. In this way, entrepreneurs prepare the company for the next generation of leadership— when teamwork and professional practices will be far more important than the efforts of any one person.**

What these leaders understand is that the more the founder or the builder of a business becomes a folk hero to the organization, the less flexible the company will be in adapting to new threats and opportunities. They know that trying to follow in a hero's footsteps can cause successors to be intimidated into inaction or to be reckless in attempting a heroic feat of their own.

Replacing a founder hero with a successor hero can lead to other problems in later generations. A hero's branch of the family too readily feels it has carried more of the load and created more of the wealth. Other family branches may begin to feel jealous of the "worship" the hero gets. The hero may come to feel either burdened or more deserving than other family members. Failure to develop a team approach can retard and limit the business's growth. People often think future leaders must have the same personality and style as the hero—just when a new kind of leadership is required.

As you prepare for letting go, you do both the family and the business a favor by fighting dependency. Even though you love it and feel needed when people ask for your opinion, advice, or direction, what you need to increasingly do is to say, "You make that decision." Or, "Why aren't you making that decision?" Or, "If you want my input, you've got to lay out some more specific options." Or, "What's the plan that you've developed on this?" People need to be independent of you for responsibility and authority, independent of you for accountability and ideas. **It becomes more important than ever before that the real responsibility and the real authority is in the hands of your people, whether they're your family members or your non-family executives. And as important, YOU must become accountable for making sure that others are being held accountable, not for doing the job yourself.**

Building a successful business is truly a heroic accomplishment. But the less the hero's personality is emphasized, the better the chance for continued family business success.

INNER DIALOGUE

Developing a Rationale

For Hanging On	For Letting Go
This company is really in serious condition. Without me, it could go down the tubes.	I've seen to it that this organization is in superb shape, it doesn't need me to run it anymore.
I have no successor. My kids are not interested, and none of the non-family executives can do this job.	My daughter is well prepared to be CEO. She has great backup in her management team.
I'm in good health, and I've got lots of energy and good ideas. I still have a lot I want to do for this company.	While I'm still healthy and energetic, I want to offer my experience and ideas to other endeavors— maybe some non-profit organizations.
I'd be bored silly if I retired.	There's so much to do in life, I'll never get bored.
As CEO of this business, I enjoy a lot of influence in the community.	I'm confident that I can still exert influence on the community even if I'm not CEO.
To tell the truth, our personal finances would be shaky if I left the business.	Long ago, my spouse and I started setting aside funds outside the business for retirement. We have met our personal financial goals.
I'm never leaving.	I'm really looking forward to the next stage of my life.

Chapter 6

The Supporting Cast

A CEO's decision about letting go affects a whole lot of people, and a whole lot of people, in turn, affect the letting-go decision. The CEO's spouse, sons and daughters, key non-family employees, and the members of the board of directors are among those most likely to be involved. They are the supporting cast in the drama of letting go, but that doesn't necessarily mean they are supportive.

TIPPING THE BALANCE

For better or for worse, spouses may greatly influence the retirement decision. One wife might be alarmed at the thought of her husband retiring. Her perspective stems from her own self-interest: "I've got my life set up the way I like it. If my husband retires, he's going to mess up my life big time. I want him to stay in the business." Another might be a real cheerleader for her CEO husband: "My husband is happy doing what he's doing. I want him to be able to continue doing what he wants to do." In both cases, the spouse is likely to encourage the incumbent CEO not to let go. She (or he) is the power behind the throne and may in fact be propping up the throne.

A CEO's decision about letting go affects a whole lot of people, and a whole lot of people, in turn, affect the letting-go decision.

Still another spouse may be concerned about economic well-being. If she thinks that her and her husband's economic welfare is best served by him staying in charge of the company, she'll advocate that he remain in charge. If she sees that her CEO husband has been making some bad decisions lately and worries that he'll run the business into the ground, she'll push him to retire before their economic security is destroyed. She may even turn to the potential successor or a non-family executive for support.

Spouses who are advocates for their children as successors to the CEO will push hard for retirement so that their children will have an opportunity to lead. Others are advocates of retirement

INNER DIALOGUE

Should I Encourage My CEO-Spouse to Retire?

Discourage	Encourage
He really loves leading the company. I can't bear to see him unhappy.	His dream has always been to continue as a family business. It's time to make that dream come true.
Maybe he's right when he says the kids aren't ready to take over.	The kids are ready; I want them to have the chance to run the business.
What would he do with his time if he retires? He hasn't really developed any interests outside of the business.	We've always wanted to travel and do some volunteer work together. Now's the time, while we still have our health.
I like my life the way it is. If he retires, he'll start to try to manage the way I run the house—a job I've done for 40 years.	He'll get impatient staying at home. It won't take him long to find something interesting to do elsewhere.
The business is thriving. Why should he quit when it's doing so well?	He's been making some costly mistakes. What will happen to us if the business fails? It really needs a fresh leader.
He should hang on.	He should retire.

because they want to do things with a CEO husband or wife that they've waited years to do: "Doggone it, let's travel before we're too old. There are other things in life, and we can't do them because you keep working."

Spouses can play a lot of different roles in the retirement decision from a number of different perspectives. Sometimes, they can be extremely conflicted about what's the right thing to do in terms of serving the business interests, serving their own interests, supporting the CEO spouse, and supporting their children.

Spouses, however, have tipped the balance by saying, "Honey, letting go is the right thing to do. I'm here. I'll support you. We'll have a great life together. It's time to move on to the next phase."

When letting go is a difficult decision, having your spouse's support—both for the decision itself and in terms of what life is about after the decision can be incredibly wonderful.

A TWO-WAY STREET

One of a CEO's greatest (yet frequently unacknowledged) fears is loss of power in the family. What happens if a family is in conflict or a family member is in need? Parents often feel that keeping control of the business and its purse strings provides extra strength in addressing potential family problems.

But succession—and letting go in particular—is a two-way street. One family business successor's insights made this very clear.

"I finally got it!" he said. "It was my *expectations* that made the power struggle so painful for me. My parents rightly were upset by my expectations of them. And the longer I held on to those expectations, the more they fought letting go."

He then described several expectations that are extremely familiar and widespread among next-generation members of business-owning families. They include:

♦ **Entitlement:** the expectation that the next generation *deserves* what the parents have.

◆ **Equality:** the expectation that parents should treat each sibling equally.

◆ **Perfection:** the expectation that the parents should take all the initiative and provide all the wisdom in letting go.

◆ **Responsibility:** the expectation that parents should straighten out conflicts among the offspring.

Parents who have these expectations of themselves or who accept them from their children inevitably face great frustration. Next-generation members who cling to these expectations retard their own growth and development.

Even as sons and daughters complain of inadequate progress toward succession, their own actions can subvert the process. Each time one sibling complains to parents about another, succession is slowed. Every time siblings need parental help to solve problems among themselves, they give the CEO parent another reason not to retire. Every time a member of the next generation asks parents for financial resources to help support a lifestyle or personal need, the parents become more nervous about succession.

Part of succession, and personal maturity, is letting go of the expectations one has toward one's parents.

When successors adopt four attitudes, they are able to let go of problematic expectations. They can then more comfortably negotiate the inevitable trials of generational transition. They:

1. Appreciate that their parents are not perfect
2. Accept parents for who they are . . . with respect and with love
3. Understand that life isn't fair
4. Assume personal responsibility for their own life, security, and identity

In my experience, **the parent's ability to cede power correlates with the next generation's ability to let go of emotional expectations of their parents.** As one successor put it, "When I assume personal responsibility for who I am and for my own success, my parents can't wait to support me. They seem to draw on my strength. It helps them."

Part of succession, and personal maturity, is letting go of the expectations one has toward one's parents.

INNER DIALOGUE

Helping My CEO-Parent to Let Go

Over-eager Beaver	Patient Preparer
I've got to get Dad out of here. I need to make my own decisions.	Maybe I should take a look at myself and see if there's something about me that's holding up Dad's retirement decision.
Why won't he just let go? It's my turn now.	I'll make sure Dad knows I understand how painful it is for him to leave this business.
If Dad would only tell me what he wants, I'd do it. But I'll want him out of here before I act.	My siblings and I need to figure out what to do on our own and show Dad what we can do.
Doesn't Dad see that I'm the one who should succeed him? Why is he stalling about announcing me as the next CEO?	I'd love to run this business, but my sister would also be a great CEO. I need to be sure Dad knows I'll support her, if she's the successor.
As soon as I'm in charge, my brother is out of here. What a loser! I don't know why Dad's been protecting him for so long.	We have to help our youngest sib see that he's not right for this business. But we'll do it with love and help him explore other options.
What can I do to make Dad retire?	It's up to us to be prepared to take charge and show Dad we can work together.

SIGNIFICANT OTHERS

Non-family executives and board members are a part of the push and pull of the letting-go process. Like spouses and offspring, they may have conflicting feelings and motives. Longtime key executives and handpicked board members are likely to be long-standing cronies of the CEO. They've contributed to one another's success, they think alike and are comfortable with one another, and they enjoy prestige and perks because of their position in or association with the company. If, in their minds, a change of leadership threatens their position, they may well discourage the CEO from letting go.

> A board can establish the policy that governs retirement for the company as a whole, helping to minimize the anguish a family goes through when a CEO is reluctant to retire or ambivalent about doing so.

On the other hand, as we saw in Chapter 3, they can play a very constructive role in determining when a CEO should let go. They can be more objective than the CEO about his or her ability to continue to lead the company. Even better, a board can establish the policy that governs retirement for the company as a whole, helping to minimize the anguish a family goes through when a CEO is reluctant to retire or ambivalent about doing so.

What a thoughtful CEO can do is lay out expectations for the board and key managers. The CEO should make it clear that board members and key managers are expected to help groom and, at the appropriate time, to make way for the next generation. The CEO should also make clear what role he or she expects these significant others to play in the letting-go process and consider making the performance of these responsibilities a part of the non-family employees' annual review and reward system. As suggested earlier, the incumbent CEO can also "layer" management so that when the new leader takes charge, there are already talented non-family managers in the successor's age group to give him or her support. In any case, treating the older executives and board members with respect, enlisting their participation in the letting-go process, and recognizing them for their contributions to the transition of the company to the next generation will go a long way to ease fears and reduce resistance to the change that must inevitably come.

THE FEAR OF MORTALITY
By Dr. Bernard Kliska

The author is a licensed family therapist and associate of the Family Business Consulting Group, Inc. Once the CEO of his family's plastic and glass container business, he relinquished his position to one of his fourth-generation sons.

Never underestimate the power of superstition. Few would dare say this aloud, but you would be surprised how many founders fear that within a year of giving up their business, they'll be dead. This fearful fantasy takes many forms. If their life's work is done, then their life is done. Their business is their life. Since a person with no goals and no challenges can actually wither away and die, their fears might really be true. We've all heard of self-fulfilling prophecies and stories of someone who hangs on until the next birthday or anniversary and then dies the next day.

I still remember a female CEO who had taken over the company when her husband died. Ten years later, two of her children could have easily taken the reins from her now-faltering hands. But to her, giving up the business was like losing her husband all over again.

Trying to disprove or reason fears away is like trying to wrestle with a ghost. Don't expect people who have held onto power and control for decades to admit to their fears. They have found a very effective way to quell and even forget their fears—by running a business. Expecting them to give this up for logical reasons does not work.

I find it useful to deal with fears not through ridicule or logic but through reassurance. Perhaps the most common mistake is to confuse being reassuring about fears with trying to talk someone out of them. **Reassurance means that you acknowledge and accept the intractability of the fear and find a solution that addresses the fear's reality.**

To reassure someone about the fear of mortality, I believe it's essential to help that individual find a new challenge, something that energizes the person and gives new meaning to his life. For example, help the retiree ease into philanthropic or volunteer work.

I see a long overdue change finally happening in our society—more people are seeing that our older citizens can impart a lot of knowledge, experience, and wisdom. I believe that this trend is going to accelerate and that people who are giving up the reins today are in a position to ride with the wave rather than struggle against the tide.

TALK, TALK, TALK

The need for dialogue can't be emphasized enough. As the "Inner Dialogues" throughout this book suggest, it is crucial for CEOs (and other family members) to have many conversations with themselves about their doubts and fears and desires as they relate to letting go.

But **it is also absolutely essential for the CEO to have ongoing dialogues with others.** Talking with a spouse, a friend, a family member, a professional, a board member, a treasured key employee, and so on will help you explore the issues that need to be explored. It will help you see how your letting-go decision affects others and the company itself. Conversations with others will help you gain valuable insight and help you shape your thinking and your plans. So keep on talking—and listening.

INNER DIALOGUE

I'm Worried about Conflict among My Kids

They Need Me	They Need Me to Leave
The kids depend on me to make the major business decisions. If I leave, there will be chaos.	They need more experience making decisions as a team. Hiring a professional to coach them might be wise.
The kids share little in common. Their perspectives and interests couldn't be more different, except they all love the business.	Diversity is good for a company! They can capitalize both on their differences and on the love they share for the business.
Talk about sibling rivalry! My sons and daughters always seem to be vying for my attention and approval. In a way, it's flattering.	I need to make sure I'm giving them each enough love and attention. Can I convince them that their individual success is everybody's success?
Their competition with one another keeps them on their toes and forces them to grow.	With some guidance, they'll see that joining forces to compete with the outside world strengthens the business and encourages their best performance.
They can't agree on anything. If I'm not there to mediate, all hell will break loose.	If I keep mediating, they'll never learn to agree on their own.
Maybe I should stay.	I should be letting go.

Chapter 7

Exit Laughing

Creating a Meaningful Life in Retirement

Nothing overcomes one's reluctance about retirement more than looking forward to having a good time. That's why thinking about what you want to do long before it's time to let go and learning more about yourself and discovering unexplored potential passions are so important. The old adage is true: you don't want to just retire FROM something, you want to retire TO something—something that engages you and makes it a pleasure to get up in the morning. Part of your letting-go responsibility is to find out what that something is. And, of course, it can be more than one thing.

Retiring TO something should enable you to depart from your business with a smile on your face and, despite your understandably mixed emotions, joy in your heart. Not only will you be doing something you want to do once you've let go, but you also know you will have some additional rewards: more flexibility in your life, less pressure, and a reduced sense of accountability.

FEAR OF THE GRIM REAPER

Time and time again, family business consultants like me hear older CEOs express the fear that if they retire, they will die.

And they tell you about someone they know who retired and in six months was gone to the hereafter.

While this fear is genuine, the facts about retirees are quite different. If fear of dying soon after you retire is keeping you from letting go, try this exercise: Make two lists of all the retirees you can think of. Head one list "Here," for those still alive, and the other one "Gone," for those who have passed away. Under the first heading, list all the retirees you know who are still alive, their age, their former occupation, how long they've been retired, and what they're doing now. Under the second, list all the retirees you know who died, their occupation, how soon after retirement they died, at what age they died and cause of death. Ask your spouse to contribute names, too. For example:

Here	Gone
Charlie, age 74, family business CEO, retired eight years, writes mystery novels, had two published.	Jasper, former CEO, died 14 years after retirement of cancer at age 80. He got serious about the stock market after the 1987 crash and sold out in 1999.
Lorna, 81, school principal, retired 19 years, volunteer museum docent and child advocate.	Hilda, college professor, died 20 years after retirement of a stroke. She was 85. Before her death, at age 72 she climbed Mt. Kilimanjaro.
Buzz, 76, family business CEO, retired 11 years, started a venture capital firm and sits on several boards.	
Carl, 69, family business owner, retired four years, and travels all the time.	Peter, business owner, died 24 years after retiring. He earned a college degree in history (his classmates claim that he had an unfair advantage since he had experienced what they were studying). He was 91. Heart failure.
Marty, 83, entrepreneur, sold her business 14 years ago, still consults to retailers and speaks at conferences. Considered a retailing "guru."	

Here	Gone
Jim, 71, physician, retired six years, and plays, plays, plays: fishing, travel, art collecting, etc.	Smitty, business owner, died one year after retirement at age 64. Had cancer before he retired.

Chances are, your list will look something like the one above. And it will probably surprise you because you'll likely discover that hardly anybody died six months after they retired, and if they did, their death was attributable to something else, not retirement.

What's important is to replace negative images of retirement with more realistic, positive ones. Successful retirement typically contains an accomplishment component. The best retirements are not "from" something but "to" something. People from all walks of life have let go of businesses or careers they loved only to create a happy, sometimes even more meaningful life in their later years. Family business CEOs who let go have faced down the fear that retirement leads to death because they know there are many, many role models that prove otherwise. Consider these examples:

◆ **Former President Jimmy Carter.** He and his wife, Rosalynn, were deeply saddened when he lost the election and they left the White House in 1981. However, the life they have crafted for themselves in the decades since—writing books, becoming involved in building homes for those in need through Habitat for Humanity International, working on behalf of peace the world over, and fighting tropical disease—has been, in the eyes of many, more significant than Jimmy Carter's life in politics. Jimmy Carter was awarded the Nobel Peace Prize in 2002 at the age of 78.

What's important is to replace negative images of retirement with more realistic, positive ones.

◆ **Charles Collat.** Although he's no longer CEO of Mayer Electric Supply, Inc., in Birmingham, Alabama, Collat continues as chairman of the business. He has settled comfortably into a spacious office about 20 minutes from the company. He has moved on to other challenges, including serving as president of the 550-member Rotary Club of Birmingham. He is also actively involved in several philanthropic endeavors, especially one he initiated with the College of Education at the University of Alabama–Birmingham, focusing on underprivileged children's readiness to start school. About a third of his time is devoted to Mayer Electric, his passion since 1953 but at last, no longer his responsibility.

◆ **Julie Andrews.** In 1997, Andrews lost her legendary singing voice to an operation for the removal of a cyst from a vocal cord. Despite her loss, Andrews, now in her late 60s, is as busy as ever, not only with acting but also with new endeavors. As this book was being written, she was getting ready to make her stage directorial debut, was preparing for the launch of her own imprint of children's books with HarperCollins, and working on her autobiography. "Not singing is very sad for me," she told a *Newsweek* reporter. "What is amazing to me, and kind of a blessing, is that I am busier than ever and it has opened other avenues for me."[6]

◆ **Richard L. Haid.** The former CEO of a family-owned insurance business, Haid prefers the term "protirement" to retirement. After letting go of the family business, he went back to school and earned a Ph.D.—exploring career development, adult learning, family dynamics, and personal transitions. Based in Hamilton, Ohio, Haid has carved out a new career for himself as an "adult mentor," helping people across the country to enhance the quality of the "third quarter" of their lives. He sees the protirement period as "potentially the most abundant time of life."

◆ **Dorothy Jurney.** A prize-winning women's editor for a number of major daily newspapers, Jurney retired at age 66 in 1975. In the years that followed, she initiated research on women in news management positions and published an annual report on the topic for ten years running in a newspaper trade publication. She was also the founding chairman of New Directions for News, a journalism think tank that has involved many notable newspaper editors. In 1988, she was awarded one of journalism's most prestigious prizes, the University of Missouri Honor Medal. She didn't pass away till she was 93, nearly three decades after her retirement.

♦ **Roy Richards Jr.** Richards was in his mid-20s when, on the death of his father in 1985, he became chairman and CEO of Southwire Company, the company Roy Sr. had founded. One of the world's largest manufacturers of wire and cable, Southwire is based in Carrollton, Georgia. Roy Jr. is still chairman of the company, but he retired from the CEO role in 2002 while still in his mid-40s. He didn't marry until he was 44. After an exemplary career at Southwire, he's now living in London with his new wife and son and enjoying a change of pace.

NEW GOALS FOR THE FUTURE

As the article by Dr. Bernard Kliska in Chapter 6 indicates, a lack of goals and challenges can be harmful to one's health, perhaps even fatal. That's why **it's so important as early as possible to start thinking about what you want to do or what challenges you want to meet once you have relinquished control of the family business.**

You can begin by simply asking yourself, "What are my goals for retirement?" That question will encourage others, such as: "How am I going to use my time?" "What am I going to find satisfying?" "How can I make a contribution to my community?"

"Successful retirement" means different things to different people. Some people think of retirement in terms of relaxation, and they immerse themselves in golf, travel, hobbies, or just dabbling in this or that. They're perfectly happy with that kind of life. Their goals might be something like becoming the best golfer they can be, or making a list of countries they want to see and then touring one or two a year. One retired business owner enjoyed researching the locations of the birthplaces of all the U.S. presidents and then visiting them one by one with his wife. If they were going to visit a relative or friend in another state, they'd make a side trip or two to see one of the presidential birthplaces.

Others see "successful retirement" as an opportunity for creating a second career or doing something that they see as meaningful and fulfilling. They go into consulting; they take directorships; they go into education or public service. They may also use the skills they have developed and focus on philanthropy and volunteerism. Many former CEOs have simply wanted to put their experience and their knowledge to use. Many also have goals related to rebuilding or re-establishing relationships with their spouses, families, and friends.

For the type A personality, a second career usually has no substitute. The retiring CEO must find other fulfilling interests. In the best of worlds, he'll search out and test these other opportunities long before it's time to leave the business.

Robert J. R. Follett is chairman emeritus of Follett Corporation, a family business known for its hundreds of college bookstores. Reflecting on what his retirement goals would be, Follett once said: "I have yet to learn to comfortably ski the really steep and deep runs. There are several 14,000-foot mountains in Summit County, Colorado, that ought to be climbed before age steals away my legs and lungs.

"Successful retirement" means different things to different people.

"I painted and sculpted as a young man. I want to see if I can still create beauty. There are books in me I want to write. There are vast reaches of this wonderful earth that I haven't seen. And somehow, I would like to find a way to express my lifelong interest in education.

"Then there is [my wife] Nancy. She has put up with me for going on 44 years. I hope that in my retirement I can repay her some of what she has given me. Her thoughtful hard work at home and in the community has made it possible for me to do what I have done so far."

INNER DIALOGUE

What Will I Do with My Time?

Hanger On	Mover On
This business has been all-consuming. I've never had time for anything else. Leaving would be like jumping off a cliff.	I've always made sure to have some interests outside the business. They give you things to look forward to when you retire.
I learned to play golf well because it was business related. But you can get bored playing golf all the time.	Sure, I love golf. But I also love fishing, hiking, birding, gardening, chess, music, and a zillion other things.
This business is the only thing that really gets my juices flowing. What would I do without it?	If I miss the business too much, I'll start another one or agree to sit on some business boards.
Things I used to enjoy before I became CEO have all slipped away. Photography, woodworking—I can't do them anymore.	I'm sure glad I kept up some of my earlier interests—especially the jazz band.
I'm too old to start learning anything new.	We're going to Italy next year, so my spouse and I are learning to speak Italian.
I'd like to spend time with the grandchildren, but we're pretty distant. I'm not much good with kids.	I'm looking forward to introducing my grandkids to new experiences.
I'm not retiring.	I've got so much to do—when will I fit in the volunteer work???

RESOURCES ABOUND

Today there are more opportunities than ever for retiring executives to find challenging, useful, and meaningful activities. Here are just a few examples:

Volunteer Opportunities

SCORE. The Service Corps of Retired Executives links retired executives with small business to provide consulting by email, phone, or in person. www.score.org or 800-634-0245.

AARP. AARP lists dozens of volunteer activities, either within AARP or with other community and national organizations. www.aarp.org or 800-424-3410.

Feeding America (formerly Second Harvest). The nation's leading domestic hunger-relief charity may offer many opportunities to help, and you may find that assisting some of the neediest members of our society is an excellent antidote for the irrational fear of poverty that so many successful founders have. www.feedingamerica.org.

For dozens of other suggestions, call your nearest volunteer office or ask your local United Way for a list of volunteer opportunities in your community or state.

Coaching

For those who want to continue to earn money, one of the fastest-growing fields is coaching. It's ideal for retired people because the training, marketing, and actual coaching can be done entirely from your home.

There are many places that offer training, but here are two where you can begin your research:

International Coach Academy: www.icoachacademy.com or 866-262-2400.

International Coach Federation: www.coachfederation.org or 888-423-3131.

EXHIBIT 4   Twelve Meaningful Things You Can Do in Retirement

1. Start another business.
2. Become an "angel" investor and support other entrepreneurs.
3. Spend more time with your grandchildren.
4. See the world.
5. Play a more active role in your church, synagogue, or mosque.
6. Write about your experiences, either for publication or for your family.
7. Teach or lecture at a local university.
8. Use your expertise to help your favorite non-profit organization.
9. Consult to other businesses.
10. Tutor and/or mentor young people.
11. Engage in strategic philanthropy—perhaps start a family foundation.
12. Build or add to a collection (art, crafts, books, sports memorabilia, etc.). Plan for its eventual donation to a museum, university, or other institution.

Chapter 8

The Post-CEO Role

Six acrimonious months after a 42-year-old third-generation leader was named CEO and president of his family's firm, he asked for a meeting with his father, the chairman. "Dad," he said, "ever since I became CEO, we've had a real problem. I make decisions, and you change them. Nobody knows who to listen to. This has got to stop." The father started to interrupt, but the son continued. "Now Dad, the way I see it, we have two jobs at the top of this organization. The president/CEO has responsibility for running the company, and the chairman travels and plays golf. I'll be happy to do either one. Your choice."

Six months later, the father had won two golf tournaments, and the business was doing fine.

After decades of leading a company, who can blame a family business's newly retired CEO for overstepping the boundaries sometimes? It's hard to shrug off the habits that come with being the one in charge. Better to think well ahead of time what your role in the company should be once you've let go of control. Will you be just an onlooker? Will you still participate, albeit in a much smaller way? Will you be "on call" when asked? Or is the temptation to exercise authority or advance an opinion so great that you can't resist, even if you're not invited?

CHAIRMAN IS A REAL JOB

The little story at the beginning of this chapter is a true one, but of course, being chairman means more than just traveling or

INNER DIALOGUE

The Post-CEO Role in the Business

Hanger In	Mover On
I still have a lot to offer. I've been in this business all my life. Why doesn't anybody seem to care about my opinion? I feel like people are avoiding me.	I have to be careful about opening my mouth. People who have related to me as the boss, including my son, who has succeeded me, tend to defer to me.
It's important for me to be around. I still catch errors and ill judgments. Other family members and longtime employees still look to me. I give them a sense of security.	But having me around creates confusion. Some people aren't clear on who's the boss. Some may even believe that I lack confidence in my successor.
After all these years, I'm entitled to stay involved.	He's earned the right to be the boss and implement his own ideas.
And I should be free to come and go as I please . . . and be involved where and when I want to be.	That makes me unpredictable and sometimes hard to reach. I'm not the greatest example of dependability, accountability, and follow-up.
Sometimes I feel unappreciated and out of the loop.	I know they honor and appreciate me. But they are busy moving the business forward. It is a new day . . . and the future belongs to the next generation. That was my dream, after all.
I'm hanging in.	I'm moving on.

playing golf. The son was simply making the point that his dad was trying to do the son's job as president/CEO, not the father's job as chairman.

The chairman's job in a family business can be just about whatever the chairman and/or the owners want to make it. **What's troublesome is how often the chairman designation is viewed as merely a title. In actuality, a family business chairman has** a crucial responsibility and a very real job. While the position involves oversight of the company, the chairman's job is not company management. The chairman's job is to manage the board of directors.

Many a CEO ponders whether to be bumped up to chairman on retirement or to continue in the chairman role if he or she has been both chairman and CEO. If you stay on as chairman, some business owners reason, you can still play a vital role in the company.

Entrepreneurs who founded, grew, and actively operated a successful business often have difficulty separating governance from executive functions. They act as their business's chairman and CEO without recognizing the distinction between the two. Having a limited, passive, or non-functioning board in many cases makes it seem that the chairman really has no job. Even when the board meets regularly, a busy CEO can see his or her board chair responsibilities as a nuisance rather than as an opportunity to use the board as a resource.

The chairman's job is not company management. The chairman's job is to manage the board of directors.

To have a "real" chairman, a family business must have a "real" board. And when a real board is developed, managing it is a real job—one too important to be left to someone who gives it secondary priority and short shrift.

An excellent board provides strategic oversight, evaluates corporate and top-executive performance, represents and relates with shareholders, serves as a resource to top management, protects and enhances the company's assets, and fulfills legal requirements. That's a lot of responsibility.

The chairman manages the process of fulfilling those responsibilities by assuring a strong, knowledgeable, fully informed board, replenished as necessary. He or she must work to develop constructive relations within the board and between the board, the management, and owners.

Not all outgoing CEOs want to be chairman. One family business founder I know had done a good job of establishing an active board. Three outsiders served with family and key employee directors for over a decade. The board was kept informed and the members' advice was valued.

This founder had also done a good job of permitting his successor son great latitude as CEO while maintaining a watchful eye. But then he did an interesting thing: **after gaining family consensus on his decision, he demoted himself from chairman to board member and appointed an outside director as chairman.** In addition to respecting his appointee, the founder felt the individual could better serve as a mentor to developing family leaders. This business owner was more comfortable with independent oversight of the sophisticated strategic and financial management needed by the growing company. He wanted new outsiders chosen for board service and vested the new chairman with the responsibility for leading that effort. **But most important, the founder felt that he wasn't very knowledgeable or good at the chairman's job and that his appointee had the experience and skill to do the job more effectively than he could.**

Excited by the challenge, the new chairman set out to revitalize board membership and process. The successor CEO was thrilled by the opportunity to work with a deeply respected, seasoned executive.

A crucial job in the family business that had not been adequately filled was now being handled by someone eminently qualified—for the benefit of generations to come.

Here's the view of a former CEO who went even one step further and declined to sit on the board at all:

OPTING OUT

By John F. Bitzer Jr.

Excerpted from a presentation made by John F. Bitzer Jr. to members of the Loyola University–Chicago Family Business Forum following his 1997 retirement as CEO and chairman of ABARTA, Inc., a Pittsburgh-based family-owned holding company. Ownership and leadership is now in the hands of the family's third generation. ABARTA operates subsidiaries in soft-drink beverages, newspaper and magazine publishing, and oil and gas exploration and development.

I thought a lot about the chairman's position and realized that I didn't want to—and shouldn't—do it. This decision meant that family leadership passed to the next generation along with business leadership, all at once. The move was described by some as highly unusual and risky . . . risky to me and risky to the organization as a whole in the sense of continuity in the eyes of our people. While I've said that this was an emotional/intuitive decision, in retrospect it seems obvious and logical for several reasons:

♦ I've never believed that retired CEOs of *public* companies should stay on the boards of their companies. It's not fair to the successors.

♦ I think that our third generation is smart and tough, lacking only in experience. But they'll get it and have a strong, experienced board to help them through the tough issues.

♦ I believe my generation learned and grew faster and became better from having the experiences and making the mistakes, at relatively young ages. That's because we were able to *control our lives* early on, and now the *third generation deserves to control their own lives*—and their results *will be their own.*

♦ I hope to set an example for the [members of the third generation] to consider so that they don't stay around too long when it's time for the next generational transition.

♦ I don't picture myself as a good director. I think I would probably talk too much and be defensive of the owner-managers in the face of tough board questioning, when they should be learning to deal with the board on their own. And while my experience will be missing at the board level in the early going, I can always be available to management.

♦ I've challenged myself to build a life largely apart from the business. It's my observation that this is the toughest part for a lot of people in this situation—to sustain a sense of personal worth without the trappings of the job and the business. This is why many stay around too long ... and it's not a good reason to do so. I think we have to look at life as holding many options and our final commitment to personal growth vis-à-vis the business is to meet the challenge of the transition ... My wife and I have places unseen, books unread, 12 grandchildren we need to know better and show the world. Some other companies' boards seem to be accepting of what an ex-patriarch has to offer, and the same of golf, which was put on hold for 22 years, awaits.

As John Bitzer suggests, there is a potential danger in having ex-CEOs serve as chairmen or even as members of the board. Sometimes they are so strongly identified with and so insistent on a particular strategy that they try to impose "the way it was" on a company as opposed to the way it needs to become.

Just as it helps to have a job description for a CEO, so is it helpful to have one for the chairman. Here is how one thoughtful family business chairman described his role:

EXHIBIT 5   Job Description: Chairman of the Board

♦ Assure that shareholders are kept adequately informed of affairs of the company and develop and maintain a shareholder relations program of the company. This includes giving thoughtful consideration to shareholder concerns and needs and reporting those concerns and needs at least once per year to the board.
♦ Be accountable, with other directors, to shareholders for proper execution of duties and responsibilities of

the board in connection with shareholder rights and interests.

- Develop responsibilities to be assumed by the company's board of directors.
- Through the president and CEO, (a) offer counsel when asked; (b) assure that board decisions are understood and implemented; and (c) assure that management has an active and effective strategic planning process.
- Keep informed on state of the company's affairs, and through the president and CEO, assure adequate flow of information to the board.
- Develop the board as a dynamic, constructive force in the company and guide it in discharging its responsibilities. Propose methods to the board to help it identify opportunities and means to improve board functioning.
- Ensure board members are knowledgeable in industry matters.
- Propose time and place of board meetings, call meetings, preside at meetings of shareholders.
- Review reports and proposals of management with officers prior to presentation to the board.
- Lead the board in preparing the annual slate of directors and selecting candidates to fill vacancies.
- Responsible for securing reliable, certified audit to verify management's conduct of the business.
- Make recommendations to committees of the board. Present to the board reports and recommendations made by committees of the board. Serve on the compensation committee.
- Maintain top-level contacts with members of the community to ensure that company is properly recognized, dealt with, and appropriately represented in community affairs.
- Identify ethical dilemmas in the company and report on those annually to the board.
- Consider leading special projects as proposed by CEO.

Roberto C. Goizueta, once the longtime chairman of the Coca-Cola Company, described the chairman's role as that of the "soul" of a company. In that sense, the chairman is the following:

- **Interpreter:** understanding the family's heritage and values.
- **Steward:** protecting those values.
- **Ambassador:** setting the tone of the business.
- **Champion:** promoting the business to its owners.
- **Reporter:** explaining to owners how the business relates to the owning family's values.

Obviously, the chairman's role is not the same as the CEO's. But for sure, chairman is a real job.

STAYING MEANINGFULLY INVOLVED

Once you have let go, there are any number of ways you can stay involved with your family's business—as long as you make it clear to everyone that you are not the boss anymore and as long as you don't interfere with the new CEO's responsibilities. One thing to steer clear of is the "corner-office syndrome"—the understandable desire to retain your old office. The CEO's office is a symbol of authority, and if the retiring CEO doesn't move out of it, confusion will reign. "Who's really the boss?" employees will wonder. "Let me just run this by Sam Sr.," one might say, even though Sam Jr. now has the CEO title.

In some cases, in order to effect a complete transition of power, it's even necessary to move the former CEO off the premises. We noted in the last chapter that Charles Collat of Mayer Electric Supply, Inc., had moved on to meaningful post-retirement activities. But for a number of years, the transition did not go smoothly. In 1994, Collat had named a non-family executive as president but remained CEO. Often, when the two men's views differed, the new president would bow to Collat's opinion.

Finally, in 2001, a task force made up of three outside members of the company's advisory board met with the family business advisor and Collat to confront the challenges of transition. The group felt that Collat's continued presence at Mayer Electric impeded needed change and development. His successor executives needed space to assert their own strategy and authority.

At the board's recommendation, Collat ceded the CEO title to the non-family president and retained his responsibilities as chairman of the board. But he balked when advised to physically move out of the company headquarters. As his daughter, Nancy Goedecke, recalls, his initial response was, "I'll be out of here immediately. They're firing me." He had devoted himself to the company's success for nearly 50 years, and now it seemed like he was being tossed aside.

Collat understood the need to pass the baton. "He felt like [the board was] doing the right thing," said his daughter, "but he had to accept it. It was like going through a grieving process. It was like a real loss."

It helped when a list of responsibilities was drawn up for Collat's new role and a salary was determined. His new duties include scouting for acquisitions and meeting weekly with the CEO. He leads the board meetings and focuses on long-term issues.

Collat calls his new off-site office "the pasture." He acknowledges that there was probably confusion over what the president does and what the CEO does. "Perhaps I had to leave physically for the fact that I was no longer around to sink in and for it to become clear who the board would be looking to for results."

Collat can see now how his departure reinvigorated a business that had suffered a loss during a nationwide recession. By removing his "shadow," he permitted the company to grow.

INNER DIALOGUE

Moving Out of the Corner Office

Resisting Retirement	Embracing Retirement
I can't believe the board is telling me to move out of my office.	As long as I sit in the "boss's office," people will continue to see me as the boss.
I've been coming to this office for more than 25 years. This is my home. I know where everything is…and I hate moving.	If my successor is to have the necessary authority and respect, it must be clear that she's the boss.
If we just announce that I've retired, people will understand, even if I keep my old office.	People are so used to seeing me as the boss, strong symbolic action is required to help people change their expectations. Maybe I should move out of the building completely.
How can I stay in touch with what's going on if I move out of my office? It's centrally located.	It's easy to keep fully informed. I can use e-mail and the telephone, and, when necessary, ask for a meeting.
I'm digging in.	I'm getting a different office.

Serving as chairman of the board is certainly one meaningful way to stay involved, but it is not the only one. Some former CEOs sign a consulting contract with the business—an arrangement that is of special benefit if the retired leader is in need of some income. It also enables the successor to specify just what he or she wants from Mom, instead of Mom imposing what she wants on the new CEO. And it offers flexibility—most retiring CEOs feel more comfortable as consultants than in salaried roles; as consultants, they don't feel they have to justify their time the way they would in a salaried role.

Another important way of staying involved is to write a history of the family business or a memoir of your years in it. Arrange to have it privately published as a legacy to the family, the community, and the business itself.

When a respected, knowledgeable retired CEO knows how to keep the proper distance, chances are the next generation of leaders will invite his input.

It's also all right to offer your ideas if you do it in a sensitive manner. Almost always, the organization feels that the founder or departing CEO has earned the right to share his or her opinions. One greatly respected founder sent memos, and every one contained what he called "a new idea to consider." All suggested doing new things or doing things in a new, different way. The memos never criticized how things were currently being done compared to how they used to be done, and employees were never criticized. The ex-CEO provided the new CEO with a copy of every memo. And while the ex-CEO always expected a response, he accepted it if it was thoughtful—even if his idea was rejected or if he didn't agree. Once he received the response, he put the matter out of his head—no more follow-up, no more pursuit. He went on to lots of other new ideas. He met regularly with the new CEO and sought feedback on whether any of his ideas were contradicting any new strategies or policies. He accepted the feedback, too.

Because he was consistent, conscientious, and constructive in his approach, he was appreciated rather than seen as meddling. And he was effective. A large percentage of his ideas were used, not out of fear or respect but because he was so often right.

When a respected, knowledgeable retired CEO knows how to keep the proper distance, chances are the next generation of leaders will invite his input. In 1996, wanting to travel and enjoy a mountain home he and his wife had built, Marvin Tibbetts Jr. retired at age 55 from Tibs Group, Inc., the Suwanee, Georgia–based company he had founded 25 years earlier. He continued as chairman and his eldest son, Mark, became CEO of Tibs Group, a provider of electrical services and power quality and technology solutions. Six years later, when Tibs Group needed a general manager for a new division, Mark convinced his father to come out of retirement for six to nine months to launch the initiative. "There was no learning curve for him," said a company spokesperson. Since Marvin was still chairman, he knew the business, and he also knew electrical contracting. He was the perfect choice for the job. What an honor for an ex-CEO to be asked by his successor to take on such a challenging role!

INNER DIALOGUE

Should I Stay On as Chairman?

Maybe	Maybe Not
As chairman, I can exert a whole lot of say-so over the direction of the business.	It's my daughter's turn, as CEO, to control the direction of the company.
I won't lose the respect of my family if I'm still chairman. And I'll still be in a good position to control what's going on in the family.	My family loves and respects me, whether or not I'm running the company or chairing the board.
I still have a lot to contribute to the business. Being chairman will enable me to be useful.	I do have a lot to offer. What other endeavors can I contribute to?
Being chairman will give me something to do with my time.	I've got lots of things to do: travel, teach, read, volunteer, write, and serve on some other boards.
I'll still enjoy the perks and prestige that I enjoyed as CEO.	The perks and prestige don't mean all that much anymore. I don't have anything to prove.
I can have the fun of the business without all the day-to-day aggravation.	Board chairman is a real job. I'd probably worry and meddle too much.
I think I'll agree to be chairman.	Being chairman is not for me.

Chapter 9

What If You Choose to Hang On?

"I'm not a dynast," said one CEO who's in his mid-70s. "My ego is not involved in believing that this business will last forever. It's not my goal to see my grandchildren taking over this business. That's their parents' concern." This owner takes pride, however, in having created wealth and having contributed to his children's prosperity. He also experiences the satisfaction that comes from knowing his offspring could make their own way even if they weren't in the family business. Even though their father has not stepped aside, the three adult children have stayed in the business. He has been honest with them about his plans to hang on, and they have made their own decisions about continuing in the family firm with the full knowledge of their father's intent.

Suppose I have not yet convinced you that letting go of your family business is right for you and you decide to stay at the controls until death or incapacitation intervenes? Then, like the CEO described above, you can hang on responsibly.

There are a number of actions you can take to fulfill your obligations to the business and to your heirs:

◆ **Clearly communicate your intentions.** Make it known to your children that you plan to run the business as long as you possibly can. Then give them the freedom to do as they wish, and encourage them to follow their hearts. If that means they decide to leave the family business because your continued control stymies their ambitions and growth, then give them your blessing, and keep the doors open. If you want them to stay in the company because you love working with them, tell them so. But make sure your wishes are not mandates. If you intend to stay in power, you are standing in your children's way, and it's only fair that they have the opportunity to reach their potential wherever they can.

◆ **Develop contingency plans.** What if, even though you expect to rule your company for years to come, you get hit by that truck tomorrow? Who will take charge? Are they prepared? You need an emergency succession plan in place that spells out what's to happen if you become unavailable to run the company. The exercise described below offers one approach, and *Family Business Succession: The Final Test of Greatness* offers a discussion and an example of contingency planning.

◆ **Clearly define your position and responsibilities.** Okay, okay, so that's what this book already told you to do if you were going to let go. But even if you stay on, your role needs to be articulated, and key positions for others need to be spelled out. You can't do it all, and there need to be developmental opportunities in your company for others or you won't be able to attract talented people.

◆ **Design a development program for your successor(s).** Even if you hang on, someone will succeed you eventually. If you want your company to outlast you, someone—your children or a nonfamily executive—must be prepared to run it when you no longer can. Another title in the Family Business Leadership Series, *Preparing Successors for Leadership: Another Kind of Hero,* offers a thorough treatment of the topic.

◆ **Keep the organization's strategy, structure, and management style updated and relevant.** One incumbent CEO was advised that he was being too aloof and not giving enough responsibility to the next level of executives, some of whom were very talented. He was, for example, making decisions about capital budgeting as his own prerogative. He was persuaded to use his management committee to determine internal capital allocations, which resulted in the development of processes that made the organization more robust and less dependent on the CEO.

♦ **Develop and clearly communicate an ownership transition plan.** You need to make plans for transferring the value of the company and the control of the company. The company's value can be conveyed in a number of ways—for example, you can gift it through your estate to your children or other family members, you can dispose of it through an employee stock ownership plan, or you can arrange with your key non-family executives to have them gradually buy you out. If the business is to be kept within the family, transfer of control is a key issue. Will majority ownership be left to a spouse, who may or may not be capable of being in control? Will it go to the son or daughter expected to take over as CEO? These are matters that need to be thought through and discussed with others. And the decisions you make need to be shared with those who are most affected by them so that they, in turn, can make their decisions about their own lives based on sound knowledge of your plans.

You may be saying to yourself that most of these points apply whether you hang on to the business or let go. That's absolutely true. In either case, you will not be around someday, and you have to prepare the business and your family for that eventuality.

PRE-MORTEM IS BETTER THAN POST-MORTEM

On approaching his mid-70s, the incumbent CEO of an outstanding business once again made it clear to all that he intended to keep doing what he was doing as long as he was effective and having fun. With both his children in the business having matured nicely, working well together, and successfully operating major profit centers, no one questioned the next generation's ability or commitment. The problem was that when Dad's exit finally occurred, a massive hole would be left in crucial aspects of the most profitable and critical aspects of the business. Everyone—the next generation, key non-family executives, and Dad (there was no board; Dad wouldn't have one)—recognized the problem. But what to do?

The answer, accepted by all parties, was to conduct a "premortem" exercise. The exercise involved a committee comprised of the two next-generation owners and four key non-family executives representing finance, operations, sales/marketing, and human resources. Dad would not be part of the deliberations, although he could serve as a resource and would review the group's output.

The committee had several tasks. First, it would develop a detailed action plan. Specifically, what were all the decisions to be made and things to be done if Dad were to suddenly exit? Specific individuals were identified with specific responsibilities. The potential impact of their father's death on the next generation was discussed so that realistic expectations would be placed on them given their ability to operate during mourning. Specific areas requiring further preparation were identified and plans responding to any needs were laid out.

Next, the group focused on the organization's structure "post-Dad." Non-family executives pressed the family executives to be clear about the roles they would anticipate playing when the father was no longer on the scene. After spending time together working through that issue, the siblings reported back to the committee. Then the committee as a whole considered what the future organization should be and whether human resources were available in-house to fill anticipated positions. One recommendation of the committee was that two new executives be hired in the father's area of the business so that they'd be trained and ready when the time came.

That led to a discussion of management philosophy. Dad was a very hands-on manager. The next generation was less so, hiring outstanding people not just as high-level staff but as actual executives with bottom-line authority and responsibility. How that change in philosophy would be implemented was a topic of considerable discussion. Changes in relationships, account-ability, and compensation that would bring about a change in management culture were discussed.

Finally, post-Dad strategy was discussed. The next generation restated their commitment to continue to own and grow the busi-ness. Expectations for top- and bottom-line growth were clarified, as were circumstances under which acquisitions might be consid-ered. Lastly, the group generated a list of key questions, issues, and challenges that would serve as a continuing agenda for the group.

The results:

- Next-generation leadership was reinforced and more firmly established than ever before. How they would be working with the executive team was made clear. And since the four key executives consisted of some hired by Dad and some hired by the next generation, they had a greater sense of working as one team.
- The non-family key executives felt valued, empowered, and more secure. They gained clear understanding of future leadership, structure, and strategy.
- The father's feelings about the exercise and its outcomes were mixed. Thinking about his exit and demise was unpleasant, but some of his peers who were dealing effec-tively with those realities gave him confidence and support. Indeed, having reviewed the committee report, he decided not to wait until he was gone to begin implementing recom-mended actions.

In my opinion, a succession process governed by an active board with experienced outsiders and guided retirement policies is still the best practice. I also respect the fact that family busi-nesses are what their owners want them to be. Finally, I recog-nize that there are many possible paths to success. The keys are having common goals, developing thorough plans, and providing effective leadership for excellent executive teamwork.

EXHIBIT 6   **The Dangers of Hanging On**

- The business stagnates because it needs fresh leadership.
- Adult sons and daughters become angry because they never get their chance to run the show.
- The sons and daughters don't feel challenged and begin to get bored.
- The most capable family members leave the business because they can find opportunities elsewhere. The least capable remain.
- The business is left a mess when the CEO dies because he has not shared information but "kept everything in his head."
- As time wears on, the sons and daughters become ready to retire before their parent does.

A succession process governed by an active board with experienced outsiders and guided retirement policies is still the best practice.

After all, a "pre-mortem" in anticipation of changes required by generational transition is a lot better than performing a post-mortem on a business that failed to survive.

Chapter 10

Summary

For most family business CEOs, the prospect of relinquishing control is enormously troubling. It presents many fears—the fear of mortality, the fear of poverty, and the fear that one's adult children won't get along. Most family business CEOs put their hearts and souls into the business for all of their adult lives. The thought of letting go and the process itself introduce feelings of grief and mourning that are natural and appropriate to one of life's major passages.

Yet, as most CEOs recognize, they must let go if the business is to make the transition to the next generation. If a company is truly a family business and the CEO desires to pass it on to his or her sons and daughters, the incumbent leader needs to give up both the CEO role and voting control.

Indeed, the incumbent CEO's attitude is a key to transition in a family business. The CEO can make or break a succession. **The process of letting go begins long before the CEO's retirement takes place, even before actual succession plans are drawn up.** An understanding that "I am going to let go at an appropriate time" undergirds the succession process. The wise CEO commits himself to that promise and turns the decision of when to retire over to others—by creating a system to establish a retirement policy or mandating that the board of directors determine when it's time for the CEO to go. The CEO does not trust himself to make that decision. He knows he cannot make it objectively;

he'll be too tempted to stay on longer than he should—past the time when he's still an effective leader.

The thought of letting go and the process itself introduce feelings of grief and mourning that are natural and appropriate to one of life's major passages.

CEOs who commit themselves to letting go prepare by making themselves secure in four areas: assuring that the company is sound enough to sustain itself without the CEO, achieving personal financial security, making sure the children really grow up by giving them the opportunity to succeed or fail without their parents' protection, and achieving personal psychological security. Letting go is an inner process that requires developing a great deal of mental and spiritual strength so that one can separate his or her identity from that of the business and understand that they are two separate entities. CEOs who let go know that even without the business, they still have worth. They learn that they can, when it's time, give up the meaningful work and rewards associated with their business in exchange for other meaningful activities and rewards.

Such CEOs know it helps to develop a rationale for letting go—one that articulates the rewards that they will gain in trade-off for the loss they will inevitably feel. They also know that it is their responsibility to plan for life after business and to develop interests that will engage them and energize them. There is, after all, more to life than just one's family business.

Letting go is an inner process that requires developing a great deal of mental and spiritual strength so that one can separate his or her identity from that of the business and understand that they are two separate entities.

It's essential, during the letting-go process, to have dialogues with yourself and with family, friends, key employees, and even professionals, such as therapists or clergy. They can help you explore and address the issues that concern you, and you, in turn, can learn more about how your plans will affect those close to you.

Despite the advisability of letting go, some CEOs decide to hang on until death or disability forces them out of the driver's seat. If you are such a CEO, you have learned in these pages that it is possible to hang on and still be responsible about it. This means making your intentions clear to those affected by your decision. It also means making the effort to assure that you have a viable company, one that can go on without you, just as the CEO who lets go must do. The responsible "hanger on" also understands that it's not fair to hang on and still expect one's sons and daughters to stay in the business. If you're not going to step aside so that they can have the opportunity to run the business, it's only right to support their desire to go where they can rise to their full potential.

For the most part, however, **the wisest CEOs embrace the necessity of letting go and the responsibility and preparation that it requires.** They find joy in knowing that they have built businesses that not only will outlast themselves but that also have been preserved for the next generation of their families. For them, that's immortality.

Notes

1 *American Family Business Survey 1995.* Arthur Andersen Center for Family Business.
2 Steinberg, Don. "The Lineup for AT&T Comcast." *Philadelphia Inquirer,* Nov. 14, 2002, C1+.
3 Lowry, Tom, Amy Barrett, and Ronald Grover. "A New Cable Giant." *BusinessWeek,* Nov. 18, 2002, 108+.
4 Steinberg.
5 Callahan, Patricia. "The Family." *Wall Street Journal,* Oct. 28, 2002, R9+.
6 Chebatoris, Jac. "Q&A: Julie Andrews." *Newsweek,* April 28, 2003.

Bibliography

Aronoff, Craig E., Stephen L. McClure, and John L. Ward. *Family Business Succession: The Final Test of Greatness.* Marietta, GA: Family Business Consulting Group/New York: Palgrave Macmillan, 2011.
Aronoff, Craig E., and John L. Ward. *Preparing Successors for Leadership: Another Kind of Hero.* Marietta, GA: Family Business Consulting Group/New York: Palgrave Macmillan, 2011.

Index

The Author

Craig E. Aronoff is Co-founder, Principal Consultant, and Chairman of the Board of the Family Business Consulting Group, Inc.; Founder of the Cox Family Enterprise Center; and current Professor Emeritus at Kennesaw State University. He invented and implemented the membership-based, professional-service-provider-sponsored Family Business Forum, which has served as a model of family business education for universities world-wide.

ADDITIONAL BESTSELLING BOOKS FOR YOUR FAMILY BUSINESS LIBRARY

$23.00
978-0-230-11100-4

$23.00
978-0-230-11106-6

$23.00
978-0-230-11108-0

$50.00
978-0-230-11121-9

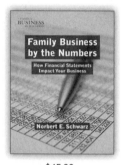

$45.00
978-0-230-11123-3

"Each Family Business Leadership publication is packed cover-to-cover with expert guidance, solid information and ideas that work."

—Alan Campbell, CFO, Campbell Motel Properties, Inc., Brea, C

"While each volume contains helpful 'solutions' to the issues it covers, it is the guidance on how to tackle the process of addressing the different issues, and the emphasis on the benefits which can stem from the process itself, which make the Family Business publications of unique value to everyone involved in a family business—not just the owners."

—David Grant, Director (retired), William Grant & Sons L
(distillers of Glenfiddich and other fine Scotch whiskey